I0123341

Deploy Predator Surveillance!

Ultimate Action Steps to Protect, *Secure or Recover Your Identity Now*

Safeguard your business and your children from Cyber Thieves!

RODNEY HOLDER

Published in the United States of America by:
FWB Publications
Columbus, Ohio

Cover Photo by
Mike McCracken

Cover Design by
1260 Productions

ISBN # 978-1-940609-24-9

This publication is designed to provide accurate and authoritative information in regard to the subject matter covered. It is sold with the understanding that neither the author nor publisher is engaged in rendering legal, accounting, securities trading, or other professional services. If legal advice or other expert assistance is required, services of a competent professional person should be sought.

-From a Declaration of Principles Jointly Adopted by a Committee of American Bar Association and a Committee of Publishers and Associations.

Copyright © 2015
All Rights Reserved

Order copies from:
Rodney Holder
P.O. Box 20463
Tuscaloosa, AL. 35402
205.310.7255 / 800.801.8855
www.DeployPredatorSurveillance.com

Preface

Does identity theft scare you? It should...

Every Day Over Forty Two Thousand People Have Their Identities Stolen!

This Could Be You or your Children!

Don't Be a Statistic; solve the problem that millions of Americans face each and every year.

If you fail to defend yourself, others will control your data: identity thieves, hackers, competitors, social engineers, and cyber spies. It is a perennial crime that has taken on new dimensions in the Information Age

This crime not only affects individuals and families, but also has costly liability implications for every business and organization (data breach, corporate espionage, reputation damage).

It's easier than you think for a criminal to get your public information and use it. To not only obtain goods and services, but also to commit fraud and even crime.

Understanding the problem is the first step to solving it.

It's not a matter of if, but when.

Don't be a victim, Read This Book, take action and protect yourself right now, before it's too late!

Dedication

I dedicate this book to the millions of you who are at a crossroads in life - who are affected by the current economic crisis and totally unaware of the severe threat of Identity Theft. I want you to know that these are, despite what they may seem, the best times to take control of your identity. I know this book will provide insight needed to secure your identity for years to come.

This book is also dedicated to my mentors, Billy and Peggy Florence, Mike and Cathy McMillan and Robert Parkerson.

A true mentor encourages us when we doubt ourselves. The more knowledge you gain the more you can experience life to the fullest. In an increasing competitive world, it is the five people you spend the most time with, the good books you read, and quality of thinking that gives an edge - an idea that opens new doors, a technique that solves a problem or an insight that simply helps make sense of it all.

They taught me to love God first and that honor, integrity, and belief all have one thing in common and that is to have them. Do not allow anyone to take these from you. A man of integrity expects to be believed and when he isn't, time proves him right. Be willing to serve others by putting other people's needs before your own. Do the right thing, be true to yourself and always believe in yourself.

Thank you for setting the example and teaching me the true values of life, to love all, trust a few, and do wrong to no one!

Acknowledgements

I want to thank my family, friends and colleagues for their enthusiasm and assistance with this project from beginning to end.

This book would have not been possible without the invaluable contributions of Randy Hardin, Savannah Helus, Tanya Skelton and Peggy Thomas whose encouragement and attention to detail helped me edit the manuscript. I owe them a debt of gratitude for their support and patience that helped me get the message of identity theft education and prevention out to millions of people around the country.

Table of Contents

Part One
Understanding the problem is the first step to solving it.

Part Two
Are your children safe?

Part Three
It's Time for a Peace of Mind

Rodney

Holder, CITRMS, CRMC

"America's Premier Identity Theft Prevention Advisor"

Rodney Holder is widely sought after for seminars, conferences and workshops. He works closely with leaders in large organizations, small businesses, non-profits and the private sector. He has traveled across the country to provide training for law enforcement, municipalities, schools, and business groups of all types. As a professional, he is informed by his belief in integrity, responsibility, reliability, commitment, competence, honor and respect. What sets Rodney apart from the rest of the industry is that while he is committed to helping your business meet multiple compliance requirements. He is trying to help you by reducing your potential liability and by educating and training you and your employees to do the right thing to protect yourselves and your customers. In today's marketplace, everyone is interested in minimizing their risk as a company. As an individual, most people are concerned about their own risk of being this crime's next victim.

The Ideal Professional Speaker for Your Next Event!

Rodney is committed to helping businesses reduce their liability associated with the information they collect and maintain and turn a potential compliance nightmare into an easy process and business differentiator. His track record and years of expertise in the identity theft arena bring additional firepower to your capabilities in fighting identity and cyber fraud. With identity theft, data protection and privacy taking a bigger role in the management of any organization, most business owners are unprepared for how to deal with it. He helps you in making the small changes that result in significant improvements to your business.

Awareness is one of the most powerful tools in the fight against identity theft, and that's where you can play an important role: The more your employees and members know how to protect their identities and what to do if a problem occurs, the harder it is for identity thieves to commit their crimes. And though these topics may seem dry and even scary, Rodney has a powerful way of not only helping your employees or members understand the problems, but to be entertained in the process. Rodney will inspire your audience to protect valuable company information as if it were their own. The result is a safer individual with strategic privacy skills that protect your organization's bottom line. By the time Rodney finishes, your audience will be fully empowered to **protect private information, at home and at work.** What are you waiting for?

To Schedule Rodney To Speak At Your Next Meeting:

(205) 310-7255

Rodney@DeployPredatorSurveillance.com

X

About Rodney Holder

Rodney is blessed to be **"America's Premier Identity Theft Prevention Advisor"**, speaker, trainer, author and a benefits coordinator. He has delivered over 2000 presentations in the area of leadership sales and privacy. Coming from a family of business owners, he understands the real challenges that owners and employees face in their personal lives. He has spent most of his professional life working through the ranks in the fields of sales and marketing and becoming a National Sales Manager (three times). He spent several years with the U.S. Chamber of Commerce helping business owners.

He holds a Certified Identity Theft Risk Management Specialist (CITRMS) and a Certified Risk Management Consultant (CRMC) designation. These are the highest credentials to be earned, held by less than 1% of the industry. He is also a Licensed Legal Services Agent. Rodney has received many national awards and honors, including the "Master of Loyalty Award" for his dedication to serving and encouraging others. He recently authored the critically acclaimed, Top Selling book, **Deploy Predator Surveillance;** *Ultimate Action Steps to Protect, Secure or Recover Your Identity, Now* and **Pearls for Parents;** *From a Single Guy with over 700 kids!*

Rodney resides in Tuscaloosa, AL. and is active in several community and business organizations. He has worked with children for over 40 years, including serving on the Board of Directors of The National Motosports Association, Youth for Christ, Kid Track International and New Beginning Christian Academy.

Okay, okay... the above statements are true, but I really want you to take the information in this book and apply it in your everyday life. It is my belief that the more educated you and your family are in regards to identity theft, the less likely it is that you, your family or your business will become victims of identity theft.

So whether you are reading this to help protect your own identity and online presence, or the reputation and sensitive data inside of your business, or to bulletproof your kids from some of the harmful forces on the web, this should get you started.

I want you to understand that identity theft and financial fraud is an issue that isn't only for the adult "ears." It should involve your whole family; from babies, teenagers, young men and women, to you, your parents, grandparents, and even 101 year young wizards.

Finally, I would like for you to have the tools that you may, perhaps, need one day to report identity theft and clear your good name. Remember, identity theft happens to even the most prepared and cautious. It is a crime of infringement on your personal identity and financial well-being. Annually, millions of cases are reported, but many are not found out until financial chaos commences.

"Please let me know if I can ever help you in any way."

Rodney Holder
P.O. Box 20463
Tuscaloosa, AL. 35402
205.310.7255 / 800.801.8855
Rodney@DeployPredatorSurveillance.com

Introduction

This is a terrific book, but I need to apologize, ahead of time, as I know that I may seem to come across as a bit aggressive in what you're reading.

My research is direct, straight-forward and I don't pull punches. My sole focus is to educate you and give you "real" steps that can instantly help protect you and your identity. And, I think you'll appreciate the fact that I'm direct and to-the-point!

My hope is that you read it, practice the guidelines and principals you find here and learn to protect one of your priceless assets, your identity.

Thieves are no longer only after your wallet, jewels, artwork or other precious belongings. Instead, they want you. With the proliferation of online transactions and the trend toward a cashless society, the number of identity thefts is on the rise. Once every three seconds someone's identity is used fraudulently.

A lot of people think about privacy but don't really care until something happens to them personally. It's like freedom. You don't appreciate it until it's gone. If you are a victim of identity theft, you experience a change of world view; you realize how little control you have over your world.

Being a victim can not only wreak havoc on your credit -- preventing the ability to qualify for a school loan, buy a house, a car or criminal charges - it can take years to overcome.

Most books on Identity Theft are written by academics, technologist or attorneys. Some take the time to show you the scams that are out there. But none of them are written for consumers or business owners to really understand what the problems are, why you should care and what you should do about them.

Deploy Predator Surveillance is written to make these complicated issues understandable to virtually anyone, helping to see why this matters to you as a consumer and as a business owner. Just as important is the fact that many companies out there are peddling offers of protection when they really don't help you at all. You don't really want to find out your product is worthless when you really need it to come through for you. Even if you choose not to follow my advice, at least you will know where you may be putting yourself at risk.

Everyone has a chance of becoming a victim. The monetary and emotional cost of repairing your identity can be extensive, requiring years to recover. In addition, the financial impact of this crime is estimated at more than $55 billion annually, impacting both businesses and consumers. Clearly, no one is immune. Identity theft happens across the spectrum of income ranges and other demographic factors.

Companies, hungry to market more effectively, mine data about current and potential customers. Government agencies make marriage certificates, housing transactions and court records publicly available - and online information brokers' package and sell that public information to anyone interested. The personal information of millions of people is compromised through data breaches.

All businesses, medical practices, organizations and schools have a responsibility to protect the personal data they collect against unauthorized or illegal use. Although the information used to commit fraud and identity theft is often stolen directly from the consumer, you can assist your employees and members by educating them on how to prevent and correct harm caused by identity theft.

Consumer trust in the information economy and digital age is crucial to the ongoing success of every business, school and organization in America.

Part 1

Understanding the problem is the first step to solving it.

"I am driven by my passion to pay it forward by adding value to others by increasing their awareness of Identity Theft."
- Rodney Holder

Chapter 1

What is Identity Theft?

Identity theft occurs when someone uses your personally identifying information, like your Name, Social Security number, your Child's unused Social Security number, or your Credit Card number, without your permission, to commit fraud or other crimes.

The FTC estimates that as many as 10 million Americans have their identities stolen each year. In fact, you or someone you know may have experienced some form of identity theft. The crime takes many forms. Identity thieves may rent an apartment, obtain a credit card, or establish a telephone account in your name. You may not find out about the theft until you review your credit report or a credit card statement and notice charges you didn't make - or until you're contacted by a debt collector.

Identity theft is serious. While some identity theft victims can resolve their problems quickly, others spend hundreds of dollars and many days repairing damage to their good name and credit record. Some consumers victimized by identity theft may lose out on job opportunities, or be denied loans for education, housing or cars because of negative information on their credit reports. In rare cases, they may even be arrested for crimes they did not commit.

It is much easier to prevent identity theft than it is to clear up the mess after your identity has been stolen by identity thieves. Identity theft prevention is something everyone needs to consider these days, with new cases of ID theft happening all the **time.**

"Identity Theft has been the NUMBER ONE complaint for FOURTEEN consecutive years and is growing."
- Federal Trade Commission -

It's The Law

Federal Law
The Identity Theft and Assumption Act, enacted by Congress in October 1998 makes identity theft a federal crime.

Under federal criminal law, identity theft takes place when someone "knowingly transfers, processes or uses, without lawful authority, a means of identification of another person with the intent to commit, or to aid or abet, or in connection with, any unlawful activity that constitutes a violation of federal law, or that constitutes a felony under any applicable state or local law."

Under this definition a name or Social Security number is considered a "means of identification." So is a credit card number, cellular telephone electronic serial number, or any other piece of information that may be used alone or in conjunction with other information to identify a specific individual.

Violations of the federal crime are investigated by federal law enforcement agencies, including the U.S. Secret Service, the FBI, the U.S. Postal Inspection Service, and the Social Security Administration's Office of the Inspector General. Federal identity theft cases are prosecuted by the U.S. Department of Justice.

For the purpose of the law, the FCRA defines identity theft to apply to consumers and businesses.

State Laws

Almost every state has Breach Notification laws in place. Each state is different. Many states have passed laws making identity theft a crime or providing help in recovery from identity theft; others considering such legislation. This link provides links to each state law. Be sure to go through the ones that are applicable to your business:

www.ncsl.org/issues-research/banking/identity-theft-state-statutes.aspx

Still Victims

When we talk about id theft it is often easy to imagine it happening to someone else, far removed from our own lives. But, unless you've been an id theft victim yourself, it is hard to fully comprehend the scope of this crime.

The reality is that id theft continues to grow, claiming new victims each day. A recent report published by Time indicates that there are approximately 10,000 identity theft rings currently operating in the United States. Each of these rings is a unique criminal enterprise seeking to find ways to commit fraud and make a profit from personal identities. The groups vary greatly in size and shape; some of the rings are comprised mostly of family members, some groups have just a couple members, while others are large and complex organizations.

Identity theft stories are an important way for you to see firsthand how someone got their identity stolen. Also it is important for people who are victims of identity theft to file "Victim's Statements" to impress upon the judge and others the severity of identity theft and the pain and suffering it caused you.

Victim of Identity Theft had $265,000 of purchases taken out in his name over 4 months - *CBS News*

John Harrison was a victim of identity theft in 2001 when a man named Jerry Phillips went on a spending spree with Harrison's identity. Phillips had +purchased a motorcycle, two cars and many items from Home Depot and Lowes and from department stores like Sears and JC Penny. When Phillips was finished he has purchased $265,000 worth of goods in Harrison's name. Jerry Phillips was caught and sent to jail for 3 years but John Harrison has spent years and is still trying to convince creditors that the debt is not his.

Computer Identity Theft - One man's ID Theft Nightmare his identity was stolen by keylogger malware on his computer - MarketWatch.com

Crouse had some $900,000 dollars taken from his debit card in six months. He eventually figured out that it was probably keystroke malware that had infected his computer and allowed the criminals to obtain access to all his online accounts and commit fraud in his name. Mr. Crouse used his computer for online banking and shopping. After he found out that he had been a victim of identity fraud he opened a new bank account at a different bank and the criminals hacked that bank account the next day using information they obtained with the malware keylogger that they put on his computer. Crouse who had a doctorate in organizational psychology had worked with the FBI and Secret Service before this but was getting turned down for contract jobs because they said his credit reports were poor and his financial debts were increasing all due to the identity theft. As of 2010 Crouse was still trying to get out of a mountain of debt and had to take a lower paying job because he lost his security clearance

Never too Young to have your identity stolen - New York Times

Gabriel Jimenez who was 25 in 2007 had his identity stolen as a child. He found out when his mother filed a tax return with the IRS, when he was 11, for some modeling work that he did. The scary thing about this identity theft horror story is that his mother notified the police, the IRS and the Social Security Administration at that time but the problems continued. Several years later she found the illegal alien who was using her son's social security number and the man asked her if he could keep using her son's social security number and he would let her have his tax refund. She told the man to stop using her son's social security number. When Jimenez went to college at Northwestern University he was denied basic utility services like gas, electricity and telephone service because they said he already had accounts. Jimenez still has credit problems from this horror story and is still a victim of child identity theft.

The FTC Annual Sentinel Study says that only 16.5% of identity theft is not detectable on a credit report.

What is Business Identity Theft?

Pretty much everyone knows about the "personal" identity theft problem. Criminals are also now getting very good at stealing business identities. The rapid rise in business identity theft now puts every business and business owner at serious risk.

Using the business' publicly available EIN, state registration records, or getting the owner's Social Security number, identity thieves can easily hijack your business accounts and business credit, and leave you with disastrous financial consequences.

The Risk to Businesses and Organizations:
Business identity theft has significantly greater consequences than personal identity theft because it not only hurts the business, but also employees, suppliers, and even customers.

Businesses have far fewer protections than consumers. Banks and creditors are not required under law to cover losses from financial accounts, payroll systems, or credit accounts. In fact, in almost 60% of cases, the business never recovers the funds stolen from their bank accounts. (Business Banking Trust Study, 2012)

Over $8 billion is lost or stolen from small businesses every year. (FBI)

- In 84% of cases, money was stolen before the fraud was detected by the bank (Ponemon Institute)
- 60% of businesses that suffer business identity fraud close their doors within 1 year! (Wall Street Journal)

The Risk to Business Owners:

As a business owner, your personal information is commonly used and is closely tied to your business. Business identity theft can destroy your personal credit and finances, and vice-versa! This type of fraud can leave you with personal debt and legal liabilities, tax consequences, and loss of personal income.

Chapter 2

What is Privacy?

Your personal information is more than your name, address and Social Security number. It includes your shopping habits, driving record, medical diagnoses, work history, credit score and much more.

The *right to privacy* refers to having control over this personal information. It is the ability to limit who has this information, how this information is kept and what can be done with it.

Unfortunately, personal privacy is lost, unknowingly forfeited, purchased or stolen every day. In some instances, we individuals can control how our personal information is used.

Doesn't the Law Defend Privacy?

The "right to privacy" is something many of us take for granted - but it's not mentioned in the Bill of Rights or the Constitution.

In the United States, unlike most developed countries, there is no overarching and comprehensive federal-level law protecting against personal information being collected and stored. Instead, the U.S. has a patchwork of laws covering different types of data protection - with separate laws for medical record privacy, financial privacy, tele-marketing, credit reporting and even video rentals.

Like any patchwork system, there are a lot of holes. With technology constantly evolving, our patchwork system of laws is often lagging behind industry innovations - and consumers pay the price.

What can you do?

The right to privacy is a hard-won, ever-evolving battlefield. Here's what you can do today to defend your rights to privacy:

- **Educate yourself.** The most important thing you can do is learn how to protect your privacy... *Read this Book!*
- **Support legislation that defends privacy.** Many of these bills happen on the state level - so get out and vote for better privacy protection.
- **Avoid companies with poor privacy practices.** When possible, don't do business with companies that fail to protect the personal information they collect on you. Take your money elsewhere - and let the companies know why.

Privacy and Data Protection: The FTC seeks out and prosecutes companies that violate Federal law or fail to provide proper protections for customer privacy, see online at: www.ftc.gov/privacy

Chapter 3

Data Breaches

A data breach is the intentional or unintentional release of secure information to an untrusted environment. Malicious or criminal attacks are the most expensive cause of data breaches and are on the rise. Data breaches may involve financial information such as credit card or bank details, personal health information (PHI), personally identifiable information (PII), trade secrets of corporations or intellectual property. Other terms for this phenomenon include unintentional information disclosure, data leak and also data spill.

Sophisticated techniques developed by a new breed of cyber-criminals intent on stealing personal data represent a growing threat to millions of Americans, a top U.S. Justice Department official told Congress.

"Skilled hackers are now capable of perpetrating large-scale data breaches that leave hundreds of thousands -- and in many cases tens of millions -- of individuals at risk of identity theft," said Rita Glavin, who heads the Justice Department's criminal division.

"Rather than purchasing goods with stolen credit card numbers, criminal organizations have recently begun to engage in "PIN cashing," Glavin said. *"They disseminate stolen financial information immediately to criminals who promptly withdraw money from ATMs all over the world."*

When we think about data breaches, we often worry about malicious-minded computer hackers exploiting software flaws, or perhaps Internet criminals seeking to enrich themselves at our expense. But the truth is that errors and negligence within the workplace are a significant cause of data breaches that compromise sensitive personal information. Companies in the computer software, IT and healthcare sectors accounted for 93 percent of the total number of identities stolen in 2013.

Data breaches are a security incident in which sensitive, protected or confidential data is copied, transmitted, viewed, stolen or used by an individual unauthorized to do so. This may include incidents such as theft or loss of digital media such as computer tapes, hard drives, or laptop computers. If this information is stored unencrypted, posting such information on the web or on a computer accessible from the Internet without proper information, security precautions, your information may be stolen. Also, transfer of information to a system not completely open or formally accredited for security at the approved level may cause loss or theft of sensitive information. Unencrypted e-mail or transfer of information to the information systems of a possibly hostile agency, such as a competing corporation or a foreign nation, can cause your information to be exposed to more intensive decryption techniques.

The Laptop / tablet vector remains the leader in incidents, but the Documents vector (printed material) is fast growing and demonstrates the need to manage both electronic data assets as well as printed documents. This vector has been trending upward for several years and is a potential contender for the incident leader if it continues. The Hacking vector remains the records loss leader, responsible for 48% of the records disclosed in the study. The Drive/Media vector is in second place with the Web vector in third.

Outsiders continue to pose the largest risk in terms of both incidents and records disclosed. When the threat actor is an insider, the incident is significantly more likely to be accidental in nature. While accidental incidents are more prevalent, they also cause the most harm of the insider incidents in terms of records disclosed.

In 65% of the cases, the data disclosed included the data subject's name, address and Social Security Number. However it happens, a security breach can compromise the personal information of your employees or members and have drastic, negative effects on your business, your mission and reputation, leaving you stunned and the world angry at you.

Whether or not your organization is actually prepared for a security breach, it almost certainly is *required* to comply with one or more of the complex patchwork of state, federal, and international laws designed to protect the privacy of personal information. While many of the U.S. federal privacy laws have been around for years and were designed to protect limited kinds of information, such as those held by banks and hospitals, the more recent *"data security breach laws"* adopted in D.C., Delaware, Maryland, Virginia and 45 other U.S. states and territories tend to be much broader and to govern any business -- whether for-profit or not -- that holds the personal information of a resident from a particular state. So, for example, if your organization holds the personal information of residents from D.C., Delaware, Maryland, Virginia, California or Massachusetts, then you must comply with the data security breach laws of each of those jurisdictions.

This year was marked by a number of high-profile data breaches worldwide. The United States experienced numerous incidents that shook the population's confidence in the ability of organizations, including the government, to protect sensitive information.

The public sector can't afford to be complacent. It's quite clear that agencies holding large amounts of personal information need to place greater value on that information asset.. They need to develop strong leadership and a culture of respect for privacy, as well as day to day policies and practices to provide trustworthy stewardship of our personal information at every level of the organization. There has been far too little focus on the fact that there are real people behind the masses of information that government agencies hold.

Information sharing: A data security risk.

The call has gone out for greater collaboration between government agencies and the private sector. However, trading cybersecurity secrets carries risks of its own. There is a need to bring private sector knowledge to government-owned databases, but giving more people access opens new vulnerabilities.

This is a complex issue and we need to work with the private sector to ensure this is progressed in a cost efficient way with the appropriate safeguards to strike the right balance of protecting the privacy of the individual and providing more cost-effective services to the general public.

Sharing information between organizations means that there are more places for unauthorized access to occur. If the push toward information sharing progresses, it will become critical to not only evaluate partners but utilize data-centric security solutions so that a breach in a partner's system doesn't compromise valuable records.

A critical starting point for preventing future security breaches (and the identity theft that can follow) is developing ironclad policies and practices for handling personal information from within the workplace.

As worldwide attention turns to data protection, both the private and public sectors will need to evaluate their security postures, review the implementation of data encryption software and close gaps where they exist.

What do State Data Security Breach Laws Require?

There are critical differences among the various data security breach laws. For instance, in most states, "personal information" means a person's name in combination with their social security number, driver's license number, bank, credit or debit card number, or taxpayer identification number; some states limit the scope of protected information to that which is stored electronically, and still others expand the scope to include medical information. But, in essence, the data security breach laws require organizations to conduct a reasonable and prompt investigation and to notify affected individuals, the state government (and sometimes others, such as credit reporting agencies) in the event of a personal data security breach. Some states do not require organizations to report security breaches that affect only encrypted data.

Moreover, and here's where it gets really important, a handful of states and territories, including California, Massachusetts and Maryland (but not D.C., Delaware or Virginia), also require organizations to take certain preemptive actions that are intended to minimize the risk of unauthorized access or use of personal information. For example, if your organization stores, owns, uses, or licenses the personal information of an individual residing in California, Massachusetts, Maryland or a state with a similar law (and virtually all membership organizations do), you must *implement and maintain reasonable security procedures and practices* that are appropriate to the nature of the personal information and the nature and size of your organization and its operations.

In essence, this means that, in order to comply with the law, you must adopt what's often referred to as a *written information security program* ("WISP").

The full impact of these laws is unclear as of yet, and the fact that only a few states have adopted them and have used not entirely consistent language when doing so, means there will be inconsistent approaches and enforcement unless the federal government can, at some point, pass a single, national law that preempts those state laws.

Beyond the steps required to try to prevent data loss and to deal with a loss if it happens, states may also regulate other aspects of keeping private data secure.

Prepare For Breaches
Prevention is a value

If your organization has not yet suffered a security breach, count yourself lucky -- the Privacy Rights Clearinghouse now conservatively estimates that a whopping 563 million records have been compromised since January 2005. But don't count for too long; instead, spend your time wisely by preparing for the worst. Doing so will help you minimize the likelihood of a breach by bolstering your security systems and policies, ensure that you comply with applicable state data security policy and breach laws (and any other applicable U.S. or international privacy laws), and establish safeguards and plans that will bolster customer confidence, both in good times and in bad.

Recently, the healthcare industry has seen a tremendous increase in breaches. The estimated cost for these breaches comes to more than $156 billion to the organizations experiencing these incidents. This figure does not include the costs that the organizations downstream or upstream may incur, nor that of the data subject victims. Further, it is a low estimate of the cost, due to the fact that 35% of the incidents did not name a figure for records lost. Given the potential business and reputational costs of a data breach, it's also important for business owners to educate their employees and have a mitigation plan in place to help them respond and recover quickly and effectively in the event of a breach.

Data breaches are a fact of life, and in all industries. Accordingly, security experts recommend that businesses have a data breach mitigation plan formulated in advance. You should also have the right processes and technology in place to spot a breach.

Six in 10 small business owners acknowledge that a data breach would compromise relationships with customers. Additionally, 38 percent said they would have a negative opinion of companies that responded poorly to a breach.

But it's important to proactively stop data breaches too. Companies must create strict privacy and security policies as well as data retention policies. Furthermore, businesses could avoid "breaches" simply by properly encrypting all sensitive information. Notably, if encrypted data gets lost or stolen, it doesn't count as a data breach or trigger consumer notification requirements.

Make no mistake, prevention and planning for a security breach can be a big and complex job, but so are the stakes. There are several quick and easy steps that small business owners can take to prevent the possibility of a data breach, they include:

- Learn and know the laws that apply to you and what they require you to do.
- Audit your security practices and how you collect, share and use personal information.
- Design and implement a privacy and security plan that complies with applicable laws, limits exposure, and increases customer confidence.
- Comply and adjust -- follow the plan, stay current on the legal requirements, and update your protections as technologies and laws change.

- Locking and securing sensitive customer, patient or employee data
- Restricting employee access to sensitive data
- Shredding and securely disposing of customer, patient or employee data
- Using password protection and data encryption
- Having a mitigation plan that offers employees an identity theft protection plan that can be swiftly implemented it if the worst happens.
- Updating systems and software on a regular basis and swiftly implement it if the worst happens.
- Using firewalls to control access and lock out hackers
- Ensuring that remote access to their company's network is secure
- Using a Secure Sockets Layer (SSL) is a cryptographic protocol for protecting information sent over networks such as the World Wide Web. SSL encrypts information at the Application Layer to ensure the safe transfer of data to the Transport Layer. Every time someone sends a packet of information — e.g., an e-mail, an instant message, a request to view a web page, or a credit card verification request — SSL encryption takes the information and encrypts it until it can be decoded at its final destination. This is a very simplified explanation of a fairly complicated process, but the purpose of SSL encryption is to prevent electronic eavesdropping while data packets travel from one place to another.

No security system is perfect. But in view of the complex patchwork of state-level data security laws (and other privacy laws), taking preventive measures to minimize the likelihood or scope of a future security breach and establishing contingency plans in case a breach occurs, is most likely to ensure legal compliance, not to mention a win-win outcome for your members, your organization, your mission, and your pockets.

"No one possesses that one silver bullet that will make us more secure. Data breach prevention is an ecosystem with lots of players, understanding the problem is a full-time job."

Chapter 4

13 Things Every Taxpayer Should Know

Identity theft often starts outside of the tax administration system when someone's personal information is stolen or lost. Identity thieves may then use a taxpayer's identity to fraudulently file a tax return and claim a refund. In other cases, the identity thief uses the taxpayer's personal information in order to get a job. The legitimate taxpayer may be unaware that anything has happened until they file their return later in the filing season and discover two returns have been filed using the same Social Security number.

Months before the IRS even began accepting tax returns this year, the agency already logged more than 641,009 tax-related identity theft incidents from the first nine months of the 2013. That's more than twice as many incidents as discovered in 2012, and more than 13 times the 47,000 found in 2008.

Here are the top 13 things the IRS wants you to know about identity theft so you can avoid becoming the victim of an identity thief.

1. The IRS does not initiate contact with taxpayers by email or social media tools to request personal or financial information. The IRS does not send emails stating you are being electronically audited or that you are getting a refund. This includes any type of electronic communication, such as text messages and social media channels.

2. If you receive a scam e-mail claiming to be from the IRS, forward it to the IRS at phishing@irs.gov.

3. Identity thieves get your personal information by many different means, including:

- Stealing your wallet or purse.
- Posing as someone who needs information about you through a phone call or e-mail.
- Looking through your trash for personal information.
- Information you provide to an unsecured Internet site.

4. If you discover a website that claims to be the IRS but does not begin with www.irs.gov, forward that link to the IRS at phishing@irs.gov.

5. To learn how to identify a secure website, visit the Federal Trade Commission at **www.onguardonline.gov/tools/recognize-secure-site-using-ssl.aspx.**

6. If your Social Security number is stolen, another individual may use it to get a job. That person's employer may report income earned by the person to the IRS using your Social Security number, thus making it appear that you did not report all of your income on your tax return. When this occurs, you should contact the IRS to show that the income is not yours. Your record will be updated to reflect only your information. You will also be asked to submit substantiating documentation to authenticate yourself. That information will be used to minimize this occurrence in the future.

7. Your identity may have been stolen if a letter from the IRS indicates more than one tax return was filed for you or the letter states you received wages from an employer you don't know. If you receive such a letter from the IRS, leading you to believe your identity has been stolen, respond immediately to the name, address or phone number on the IRS notice.

8. If your tax records are not currently affected by identity theft, but you believe you may be at risk due to a lost wallet, questionable credit card activity, or credit report, you need to provide the IRS with proof of your identity. You should submit a copy of your valid government-issued identification — such as a Social Security card,

driver's license, or passport — along with a copy of a police report and/or a completed Form 14039, Identity Theft Affidavit, which should be faxed to the IRS at 978-684-4542. As an option, you can also contact the IRS Identity Protection Specialized Unit toll-free at 1-800-908-4490. You should also follow FTC guidance for reporting identity theft at www.ftc.gov/idtheft.

9. Show your **Social Security** card to your employer when you start a job or to your financial institution for tax reporting purposes. Do not routinely carry your card or other documents that display your Social Security number.

10. For more information about identity theft — including information about how to report identity theft, **phishing and related fraudulent activity** — visit the **IRS Identity Theft and Your Tax Records** page, which you can find by searching "Identity Theft" on the **IRS.gov home page.**

11. IRS impersonation schemes flourish during tax season and can take the form of e-mail, phone websites, even tweets. Scammers may also use a phone or fax to reach their victims. If you receive a paper letter or notice via mail claiming to be the IRS but you suspect it is a scam, contact the IRS at www.irs.gov/contact/index.html to determine if it is a legitimate IRS notice or letter. If it is a legitimate IRS notice or letter, reply if needed. If the caller or party that sent the paper letter is not legitimate, contact the Treasury Inspector General for Tax Administration (TIGTA) at 1-800-366-4484. You may also fax the notice/letter you received, plus any related or supporting information, to TIGTA. Note that this is not a toll-free FAX number 1-202-927-7018.

12. While preparing your tax return for electronic filing, make sure to use a strong password to protect the data file. Once your return has been e-filed, burn the file to a CD or flash drive and remove the personal information from your hard drive. Store the CD or flash drive in a safe place, such as a lock box or safe. If working with an accountant, you should ask them what measures they take to protect your information.

13. If you have information about the identity thief that impacted your personal information negatively, file an online complaint with the Internet Crime Complaint Center (IC3) at **www.ic3.gov**. The IC3 gives victims of cybercrime a convenient and easy-to-use reporting mechanism that alerts authorities of suspected criminal or civil violations. IC3 sends every complaint to one or more law enforcement or regulatory agencies that have jurisdiction over the matter.

Content provided by the Internal Revenue Service. Consult your financial or tax adviser regarding your individual situation.

Chapter 5

Crucial Identity Theft Prevention Tips

Prevention vs Restoration

It takes about 60 seconds to find out that you are a victim of identity theft...

It takes an average 600 hours to restore your identity!

However, the FTC qualifies this estimate by noting that most of the actual work of identity theft recovery — phone calls, written correspondence, keeping track of creditors, responding to letters, working with credit bureaus and law enforcement agencies, etc. — involves the victims making sure that they won't be liable for the debts thieves create in their names.

1. BEFORE MAKING A FINANCIAL TRANSACTION, LOOK FOR TWO THINGS THAT TELL YOU A WEBSITE IS SAFE: One: The letters "HTTPS" -- S for "Secure" -- at the beginning of the URL, or web address. **Two:** A closed yellow padlock, either next to the URL box, or at the bottom of the screen. (Note that the 'S' may not appear until you move to the "order" page on the website.)

2. SHRED FINANCIAL DOCUMENTS: Any paperwork with personal information should be put through a shredder before being thrown away. Assume that any document you throw out will end up in the hands of an identity thief. Get in the habit of either chopping or locking documents and disks that contain identity (name, phone number, address, social security number, account numbers, client information, children's information, etc.). For best results use a mechanical cross cut or Department of Defense (DOD) approved shredding device.

3. NEVER CLICK ON LINKS IN UNSOLICITED E-MAILS: Since "phishing" is becoming a common problem, use up-to-date firewalls, anti-spyware, and anti-virus software to protect your home computer. Good anti-spam software is a must. Plus, never click on links in e-mails. Instead, open a new window and go to the website address you know in order to enter information. (Fake PayPal e-mails are becoming more common, so be extra wary when dealing with these.) You might also want to avoid e-mail archiving in the event that someone hacks into your account.

4. DO NOT USE OBVIOUS PASSWORDS: These include your birth date, mother's maiden name, or the last four digits of your Social Security number. *(See page 41)*

5. DO NOT GIVE OUT PERSONAL INFORMATION: Whether over the phone, through the mail, or over the Internet, don't share your information unless you know who you are dealing with.

6. PROTECT YOUR SOCIAL SECURITY NUMBER: Never carry your social security number in your wallet or write your social security number on a check. Did you know you can lock down your Social Security Number to prevent thieves from filing your taxes early? It won't help other forms of ID theft, but it stops this. *(See page 80)*

7. KEEP YOUR PERSONAL INFORMATION IN A SECURE PLACE: This is especially important with roommates, outside help, or if you are having work done in your home. A majority of our most valuable identity documents (passports, birth and death certificates, wills, trusts, deeds, brokerage information, passwords, health records, etc.) are exposed to identity theft (and natural disasters, such as fire and floods) as they sit in unlocked filing cabinets, banking boxes in the basement, office drawers or out in the open, on our desks. Purchase a fire-resistant (and possibly flood resistant) safe that will allow for the protection of your physical identity assets. These safes come in all sizes and shapes. Some are meant for the home and some are meant for businesses.

8. BE ALERT TO BILLS THAT DO NOT ARRIVE WHEN THEY SHOULD: If they do not arrive, they may have been routed somewhere else.

9. BE PROACTIVE ABOUT UNEXPECTED CREDIT CARDS OR ACCOUNT STATEMENTS: If an account or credit card arrives that you did not open/activate, someone else did. Call the company immediately and have it closed/canceled.

10.BE ALERT FOR CREDIT BEING DENIED UNEXPECTEDLY: Credit is often denied for a variety of reasons, one of which is when too much credit is opened in a short period of time. Being denied credit may mean that someone else has opened accounts in your name.

11. RESPOND IMMEDIATELY TO CALLS OR LETTERS ABOUT PURCHASES MADE: Credit card companies create a profile of their clients detailing out the most common places a customer shops and the items that they frequently buy. If something is purchased that does not suit your profile, they will contact you for verification. Respond to the notice right away to head off potential theft and damage to your credit.

12.CHECK YOUR CREDIT REPORT: Any credit opened in your name will show up on your credit report. By staying on top of this, you will be able to stop identity theft before too much damage occurs.

13.REGULARLY REVIEW YOUR FINANCIAL STATEMENTS: Look for any charges that you did not make.

Consumers usually have only 30 days to dispute items they did not authorize.

14.CLOSE ANY ACCOUNTS THAT HAVE BEEN TAMPERED WITH OR ESTABLISHED FRAUDULENTLY: Get a new card with a new number and close the old card, since this alone may stop a thief in possession of your information.

15. GO PAPERLESS: You can receive many of your bills through your e-mail/online banking instead of having them mailed. By requesting this benefit, you keep account numbers and personal information private. You are also able to save hard copies directly to your hard drive, which allows you to find the information quickly and easily when needed.

16.STORE YOUR FINANCIAL AND PERSONAL INFORMATION IN A STORAGE BOX BY YEAR: This is especially important when dealing with taxes since the IRS can demand to see evidential proof of deductions for as long as eleven years after you file. By keeping it in a storage box, you can shred the contents when the time period is up. Note: this does not include social security numbers.

17.BE ALERT WHEN RESPONDING TO E-MAILS: E-mails are now commonly used to steal or "phish" information out of consumers by making the e-mail look as if it came directly from a financial institution. If you respond to the e-mail, you encourage them to continue trying to get personal information from you. Simply add the address to your spam list to keep them from contacting you in the future. Visit the addresses you know if you are concerned the notice is valid.

18.WHEN CONTACTED BY AN INSTITUTION BY PHONE, TELL THEM YOU WILL CALL THEM RIGHT BACK: Let them give you their name and number, but do not call that number back. Instead, call the number on the back of your card and ask to speak to a representative about your account. Let them know that you were contacted and ask them to verify any problems. All account managers have access to the same information, so they will be able to see if there is a problem with your account or not.

19. OPT OUT OF PRE-APPROVED CREDIT OFFERS: To minimize the amount of your personal information bought and sold on the data market, begin **"opting out"**. Opting out is the process of notifying organizations that collect your personal information to stop sharing it with other organizations. By doing so, you lessen the amount of mail that comes to your mailbox, and you will still be able to apply for credit online. You can easily opt out by calling 1-888-567-8688 or visiting www.OptOutPreScreen.com

20. GET A LOCKING MAILBOX: This is an especially good idea for anyone in a nice area. The nicer the area you live in, the more ideal a target you make to an identity thief because they assume you have more money for them to steal.

21. COPY ALL OF YOUR CREDIT CARDS AND SAVE THEM IN A FILE AT HOME: By having a copy of the card (front and back) in a locked filing cabinet or other safe place, you will be able to quickly and easily contact your creditors should your purse or wallet ever be stolen.

22. CARRY ONLY ONE OR TWO CARDS AT A TIME: Lock away all the other cards in a safe place and carry as few cards as possible. This way, if someone ever gets into your wallet or purse, you will notice immediately if a card is stolen and be able to report it right away. Protect your personal information against technologically savvy thieves by using a RFID blocking credit card sleeve to cover your cards. *(See page 166)*

23. INVEST IN IDENTITY THEFT PROTECTION: An Identity Theft plan will provide you with peace of mind by leveraging experts, experience, and technology to monitor, protect, and restore your identity. Find one that offers all of the following areas of coverage for Complete & Secure Protection: Member, Spouse and Children Covered, Triple Bureau Credit Monitoring, Character & Criminal, Credit Monitoring with Activity

Alerts, Credit Report with Score & Credit Analysis, Credit Report Consultation. Consultation to Help Prevent Identity Theft,

Total Identity Restoration Services,
Offices Worldwide with Licensed Fraud Investigators
with a limited Power of Attorney,
Combined with a Legal Access Plan.

In any event, the old axiom about medicine applies to identity theft as well: An ounce of prevention is worth a pound of cure. The best way to avoid a long and painful process of restoring your identity is to take steps to ensure that your identity is never stolen.

Chapter 6

I'm a Victim of Identity Theft. What Should I Do?

As a victim of identity theft you are guilty until proven innocent. Access to legal advice, an attorney or a legal services plan may be critical.

Keep a log of all contacts and conversations with the authorities and financial institutions including dates, times, names, and phone numbers. Also note time spent and any expenses incurred. Confirm conversations in writing and send correspondence by certified mail. Keep copies of all letters and documents.

Create an Identity Theft Report

If someone has used your Social Security number (or your children's social security numbers) to file an income tax return, get a job or to obtain credit, your first step is to alert the authorities as soon as possible and advise them that you have been the victim of identity theft. You should also put a credit freeze and a credit alert on all credit reports.

Identity theft is one of the hardest crimes to protect against, for both citizens and the government. Many victims are usually in the dark, at least at first, that they have been targeted. If someone is fraudulently using your social security number, you might receive notices from the IRS or changes to refund claims.

If you have been a victim of identity theft or you suspect you may be a potential victim of fraud, besides following the steps above, you should also fill out IRS Form 14039, an Identity Theft Affidavit, which informs the IRS that someone has used your Social Security number. The form advises the IRS that your current and future income taxes may be impacted and allows the agency to mark an account to identify future questionable activity.

Upon completion of the form, you will be required to submit documentation such as a passport, driver's license, social security card, or another federal or state-issued government ID card to prove to the IRS that you are who you say you are.

This report will help you resolve problems with credit reporting companies, debt collectors, and businesses that allowed the identity thief to open new accounts in your name. The report can help you:

- Get fraudulent information permanently removed from your credit report
- Prevent a company from collecting debts that result from identity theft or selling the debts to others for collection
- Get an extended fraud alert put on your credit report

How to create an Identity Theft Report:

1. File an identity theft complaint with the FTC.
Online: http://ftc.gov/idtheft
Phone: 1-877-438-4338

2. When you file your complaint with the FTC, get a copy of the FTC affidavit that shows the details of your complaint. The online complaint site explains how to print your completed affidavit. If you file your complaint by phone, ask the counselor how to get a copy of your affidavit.

3. Take your completed FTC identity theft affidavit and go to your local police, or the police where the theft occurred, to file a police report. Get a copy of the police report or the report number. Your FTC identity theft affidavit **plus** your police report makes an Identity Theft Report. Send copies of the Identity Theft Report to companies where you report fraud. Ask them to remove or correct fraudulent information in your accounts

4. Credit Bureaus- Immediately call the Fraud units of the three credit reporting companies Experian, Equifax, and TransUnion. Report the theft of your credit cards or numbers. Ask that your account be flagged. Also, add a victim's statement to your report, up to 100 words ("My ID has been used to apply for credit fraudulently. Contact me at 555-123-4567 to verify all applications.") Be sure to ask how long the fraud alert is posted to your account and how you can extend it if necessary. These measures may not entirely stop new fraudulent accounts from being opened by an imposter. Ask the credit bureaus in writing to provide you with free copies of your credit report.

Ask the credit bureaus for names and phone numbers of credit grantors with whom fraudulent accounts have been opened. Ask the credit bureaus to remove inquiries that have been granted due to the fraudulent access.

5. Creditors/Credit Cards- Contact all creditors with whom your name has been used fraudulently - by phone and in writing. Get replacement cards with new account numbers for your own accounts that have been used fraudulently. Ask that the old accounts be processed as "Account closed at consumers' request." Carefully monitor your mail and credit card bills for evidence of new fraudulent activity. Report it immediately to credit grantors.

6. Stolen Checks- If you have had checks stolen or bank accounts set up fraudulently, report it to the check verification companies. Place stop-payments on any outstanding checks that you are unsure of. Cancel your checking and savings accounts and obtain new account numbers. Give the bank a secret password for your account.

7. ATM Cards- If your ATM or credit card has been lost, stolen or compromised; get a new card, account number and password. Do not use your old password/PIN number. When creating a password /PIN number, don't use common numbers like the last four digits to your social security number or your birth date. Avoid using ATM machines in convenience stores, bars, and/or airports. Always check the card reader for signs of tampering and never expose your password or PIN number. If you have not received a card you were expecting in the mail, find out where the card was sent.

8. Fraudulent Change in Address- Notify your local Postal Inspector if you suspect an identity thief has filed a change of address with the post office or has used the mail to commit credit or bank fraud. Notify the local Postmaster for the address to forward all mail in your name to your own address. You may also need to talk to your local mail carrier.

9. Social Security Number Misuse- Call the Social Security Administration to report fraudulent use of your Social Security card number. As a last resort, you may request a new number. However, the SSA will only change it if you fit their fraud victim criteria. Also, order a copy of your Earnings and Benefits Statement and check it for accuracy.

10. Passports- If you have a passport, notify the passport office in writing to be on the lookout for anyone ordering a new passport fraudulently.

11. Driver's License- You may need to change your driver's license number if someone is using yours as identification on bad checks. Call the Department of Driver Services to see if another license was issued in your name. Place a fraud alert on your license. Go to your local DDS office and request a new number. Also, fill out the DDS complaint form to begin the fraud investigation process. Send supporting documents with the complaint form to the nearest DDS office.

12. Law Enforcement- Report the crime to the law enforcement agency serving your area. Give them as much information as possible. Get a copy of your police report as soon as it is available. Keep the report number handy in order to give it to your creditors and others who may require verification of your case. Credit card companies and banks may require you to show the report to verify the crime.

13. False Civil and Criminal Judgments- Sometimes victims of identity theft are wrongfully accused of crimes committed by the imposter. If a Civil judgment has been entered in your name for actions taken by your imposter, contact the court where the judgment was entered and report that you are a victim of identity theft. If you are wrongfully prosecuted for criminal charges, contact the State Department of Justice and the FBI. Ask how to clear your name.

14. Legal Help- You may want to consult an attorney or invest in a Legal Access Plan to take legal action against creditors and/or credit bureaus if they are not cooperative in removing fraudulent entries from your credit report or if negligence is a factor. Call the local Bar Association to find an attorney who specializes in Consumer Law and the Fair Credit Reporting Act.

Chapter 7

Protecting Your Wireless Network

Wireless networks have attained a de facto presence in home and small business environments during the past few years. The ever increasing ability (digital phones, personal handheld devices, gaming consoles, etc.) to connect to the Internet via a wireless node has propelled the wireless network router to a place of common acceptance in the home. Small businesses often reduce costs by using wireless laptop computers in place of (or in addition to) standard desktop computers. More recently, printers have included wireless connectivity, allowing the user to place the printer in a convenient location and still make it available to a network or single user. The convenience brought to users by the wireless connection is often significant. Unfortunately, so is the increased risk of hacking if the wireless network is not secured properly. Below are some considerations to improve your security when operating a wireless network:

- **Wireless Setup:** Wireless routers are often supplied with default settings that allow a user to quickly create an operating wireless network. However, until recently, these default settings did not adequately address security issues. This has changed with some manufacturers, so that the setup utility provides instructions to secure the network. It is still an excellent idea for the user to become familiar with the router setup, and verify that the settings are applied for appropriate security, especially if the user did not do the initial installation setup.

- **Important Default Settings:** The factory default user name and password for access to most routers is well known publicly, and can easily be found by doing a web search. So is the default

SSID, the name that is publicly broadcast by the wireless transmitter to identify your network to any client computer that wishes to connect to your network. Resetting a router to the factory default settings is usually no more than depressing a back panel switch with a paper clip and rebooting the router. Here are some points that should always be checked:

- Always reset the administrator password (and the administrator user name, if possible).

- Always reset the SSID to a new name. It is also smart to pick a name that does not identify your family or business, since the SSID will (unless you make other changes) be visible to any wireless unit within range. A default SSID, like "Linksys" begs hackers to test your network, to see if any of the default login information is also being used for administrator access.
- Disable remote management of the router, unless you really do need to change router settings from a remote location.
- Ensure that the router firewall is enabled.
- Ensure that wireless encryption is enabled. All wireless devices that connect to your network must use the same type of encryption, such as WPA, WPA2, WEP, etc. If at all possible, use one of the newer standards, such as WPA2, or WPA, which are much harder to decrypt/hack than the earlier WEP standard.

- After setting a wireless "key" for the router, protect it. It is the password that will allow anyone in range of your wireless transmitter to easily join your network. A wireless client is "inside" the protection of your router's firewall in most cases.
-See that a software firewall is running on each computer in your network, both those with wired and wireless access to the network. Windows firewall is available to most users, and most good antivirus packages include such a firewall (which replaces the Windows Firewall).

- **Additional Security Measures:** The measures above should be done in all wireless network installations. Below are some actions that can be done if you have a more serious need for securing your wireless network:

- Use a MAC address access list. All wireless clients have a unique "MAC" address number, which is specific to that particular unit. Many routers have the ability to restrict access to a list of known MAC addresses. This restriction is not a "save all" method, since MAC addresses can be faked by some types of hacking software.

- If possible, locate the router in a central part of the home or business. In addition to providing the best average coverage for your intended client wireless devices, this also limits the exterior coverage of the wireless transmitter. This decreases the possibility that an unauthorized user will be physically near enough to query your wireless network. A wireless router in a second story window can be accessible from several hundred feet away, or even further if a directional antenna is being used by the interloper.

- Instead of letting the router assign IP addresses automatically to the intended clients (DHCP), set the router to accept a small range of static IP addresses. Then configure each intended wireless client with a fixed (static) IP within the range you chose. You can also choose an IP range that is private, such as 192.168.4.xxx or 10.0.0.xxx, to further prevent direct connections to the client machines from the Internet.

- Turn the router off when you will be away for an extended time. Most routers will reboot in a minute or two. Most wireless clients that were previously connected to the wireless network will reconnect automatically when the router becomes available again.

- **Choose a qualified supplier:** There are many companies that build or rebrand wireless routers. I believe it is worth your time to check online to see if the router model you are considering provides a thorough user manual. You should be able to download a PDF user manual that is thorough in explaining the setup and operation of your intended purchase, especially the security, encryption, and firewall settings available to you to protect your network. If you cannot find a thorough user manual which explains the router security settings in plain English, you would be better served to look for a different manufacturer. Ultimately, your network security will depend upon both the features available in your wireless router and clients, and the choice of appropriate settings to secure the network.

- **Defend your computers:** A secure wireless network will do little good if your client computers are open to viruses, malware, pop-ups, and other threats that can be imported through your firewall by ordinary web browsing and email. Antivirus and personal firewalls must be enabled. Operating system and antivirus programs must be updated automatically with patches and new virus definitions. An infected computer can allow system takeover, keystroke logging, and other hacking from within your network.

Chapter 8

Protecting Your Online Identity...
Cybercrimes

Cybercrime is one of the most lucrative illegal businesses of our time, and it shows no signs of slowing down. Over the last decade, cybercriminals have developed new and increasingly sophisticated ways of capitalizing on the explosion of Internet users, and they face little danger of being caught. Meanwhile, consumers are confronted with greater risks to their money and information each year.

The need to protect your identity online has become increasingly important with the growing number of social networking and blogging sites available. Personality profiles and blogging about personal experiences creates a public record of your personal information. Once it is posted – it's nearly impossible to pull back.

Computers, tablets, and smartphones have become such an important part of our lives — for accessing information, keeping in touch with friends and family, shopping, working, and other activities — that it's easy to overlook the risks of using them. We rely on computers so much that many of us neglect the importance of PC security to keep our passwords, credit card numbers, and other personal information safe from identity thieves.

The Secret Service has trained some 1,400 state and local law enforcement officers on cybercrimes since the agency started the education program in 2008. But the demand for training is greater than the agency can provide.

According to the Justice Department, if a computer is hacked, you can call your local FBI office or the Secret Service or the Internet Crime Complaint Center, which is run by the FBI and the nonprofit National White Collar Crime Center.

For Internet fraud and spam, you can call your local FBI office, the Secret Service, or file an online complaint with the Federal Trade Commission or the Securities and Exchange Commission. There are also Secret Service-led Electronic Crimes Task Forces in 29 cities, and they regularly work with state and local law enforcement.

But figuring out which task force or which federal investigative agency to turn to can be a challenge. Not everyone will have the expertise to know what time of crime occurred so that the right agency can be contacted.

That leaves few options for a victim of a cybercrime whose loss would be considered small by the federal government but crippling to the individual or small business.

Social networking is immensely powerful and is here for the long run, but we must learn to harness and control it. So whether you are reading this to help protect your own online presence, or the reputation and sensitive data inside of your business, or to bulletproof your kids from some of the harmful forces on the web, this should get you started.

Online Harassment

We're human, so exchanging salty words online is bound to happen. It's a bad idea for adults and children to respond to and potentially escalate harassment. It's even more important to keep personal information out of the hands of strangers. No one needs to know where you live or your phone number. When registering for social networking sites, don't include your personal e-mail. However, if an incensed cyberbully manages to uncover your email or worse yet, your address – record and save any threats made against you, then contact local law enforcement , as well as the service the bully is using to attack you, and report his or her behavior. Laws dealing with online harassment vary; it is important to discuss the matter with an attorney who knows the laws in your state or province.

Passwords

Protecting your digital identity has become a new challenge. Getting hacked is becoming an internet rite of passage. The growing painful password problem is twofold: Hackers have gotten very good at what they do, with more capable tools than ever, and those tools can work so well because we are still really bad at choosing and remembering passwords.

Coming up with a password is a compromise between security and convenience. Very complex passwords are highly secure, but difficult to remember. To make them work, users end up in a constant state of resetting forgotten passwords or writing them down on sticky notes. Simpler passwords are easier for us to remember, but all too easy for others to discern.

Anyone with a password that can be found in the dictionary, even if it's a slight variation followed by a number, gets found quickly.

It's possible that more than one or more of your passwords has already been stolen (you can check www.PwnedList.com, an online database with more than 966 million compromised passwords on file), but even if it hasn't, relying on weak passwords is a fools game. Once hackers get into an account, they immediately start searching for any linked or related accounts. Before long, a complete stranger could be wreaking havoc on your social reputation, credit rating, and finances. If you expect one of your online accounts has been hacked, immediately change the passwords you have on any other important account you have; hackers have programs designed to try the cracked password at other sites. Even if you've been smart enough to maintain separate passwords for different accounts, hackers will leverage access to your email to reset passwords at other sites. Forgot your password? Have a new one sent to your email account. But when you do reset your passwords don't repeat mistakes of the past. There are ways to make passwords both secure and memorable.

So what makes a good password? Using upper and lower cases, symbols, and numbers does matter. These tactics increase entropy (a measure of how random and guessable your passwords are), as well as the time it takes for a program to crack your password with brute force. You can check your passwords' "crackability" at security firm Gibson Research Corporation's site by clicking Password Haystacks at grc.com

To make a password more secure, add special characters in unpredictable places and increase the length, which is the most important factor in password strength. For example, !!!Lepoard???? would take over fifty years in an offline attack, and many more years online, despite having no numbers. So when picking a password with up to 14 characters allowed, use all 14 characters.

The No. 1 password rule is to use a unique password for each of your logins. A unique password is hard to crack and hard to hack, even if it's leaked by one website.

This brings us to another challenge: We use a lot of password-protected online services. It seems like a herculean task to come up with a strong and unique password for each one—and remember them all.

There are two schools of thought on this problem. You can use a password management tool, such as LastPass or KeePass, to generate a long, complex password for each site and remember every one for you, leaving you with only one (hopefully very secure) master password to recall. Or you can use a unique pass phrase for each of your log-ins, avoiding the off-chance that you completely lock yourself out of all of your accounts if you forget the master password.

For a pass phrase to be effective, though, it needs to be not only long and memorable, but also difficult to guess by others (even those who know you). That means generating random pass phrases (using a tool like Diceware or the xkcd Password Generator) or picking arbitrary words (as arbitrary as your subconscious allows). You can make a pass phrase even more secure by adding special characters, as in correcthorseb@tterystaplE. To account for the need to have a unique phrase for each site, include a clue to the site name. For example, for Facebook, correcthorsebatterystaplE@zuck; for Gmail, correcthorsebatterystaplE@envelope.

Password managers offer some convenience, such as auto-filling forms for you and generating and managing a ton of truly random passwords. But if you don't have access to the app or can't remember the master key, you can't log in, and if the password-manager database is hacked, all of your passwords are now offered up on a plate.

Web Tracking
The private browsing mode of most browsers prevent cookies and blocks local storage of your browsing history – but that won't stop sites from tracking your via you IP address.

I suggest the following tips to protect your identity online:

- Use the highest level privacy settings that the site allows. Do not accept default settings.
- Read privacy and security policies closely – know what you're getting into. Some major social networking sites actually say they will use or sell information about you (not individual data necessarily, but aggregate information based on your personal information and that of others using their site) in order to display advertising or other information they believe might be useful to you.
- Use the least amount of information necessary to register for and use the site. Be careful when picking a screen name – make sure it doesn't provide clues to your "identity".
- Create a strong password and change it often. A strong password should be more than 12 characters in length, and contain both capital letters and at least one numeric or other non- alphabetical character. Use of non-dictionary words is also advised. Do not share your password with others.
- Be wise about what you post. Never post personal information such as your address, phone numbers, e-mail address, driver's license number, Social Security Number (SSN), birth date, birth place, school's name, or student ID number. When blogging, do not disclose your location for any given day or the exact location for an event you are going to attend.
- Be careful when posting photos. Make sure they do not provide clues – such as where you live, work or go to school. Also, do not post photos depicting negative behaviors – including drinking, provocative poses or illegal activities. While you may attempt to delete the photo at a later time, it will continue to exist in the cyber world.
- Only connect to people you already know and trust. Don't put too much out there – even those you know could use your information in a way you didn't intend.
- Verify emails and links in emails you supposedly get from your social networking site (e.g. the recent Facebook scam emails that asked customers to re-set their passwords). These are often designed to gain access to your user name, password, and ultimately your personal information.

- Install a firewall, reputable anti-spam and anti-virus software to protect your information-- and keep it updated.

Botnots

A "bot" is an infected computer controlled by a hacker, who can use the computing power of the infected machine to perform all sorts of illegal and destructive acts. A "botnet" is a network of infected computers remotely controlled by a hacker, who uses them to commit identity theft and a wide range of other crimes.

A bot can also be a type of computer virus or malware that turns computers into bots so that a hacker can remotely control them. Botnets are a relatively new and growing threat to computer users around the world.

The criminals who create and use botnets to turn computer users into unsuspecting identity theft victims are becoming increasingly sophisticated. With a few keystrokes, the authors of botnets, called "bot-herders" or "botmasters," can harness an enormous amount of processing power and wreak havoc on a grand scale.

Most owners of computers enslaved by botnets have no idea that their machines are infected. It might seem a bit slower, crash occasionally, or display a seemingly random string of characters on the screen, but the botmasters want owners of the machines enslaved in their botnets to remain oblivious to the fact that they're identity theft victims.

Bots are spread by other bots, programs that are constantly searching for weaknesses in home and business computer networks. Using the computing power of the botnet, they're capable of millions of "sniffs" per second in their search for security weaknesses. When they find a way into a new host, they infect it, scour it for personal information, and add its computing power to the botnet.

Botnets are capable of several different kinds of crimes, including the following:

45

- Sending e-mail spam, computer viruses, and a wide range of others kinds of malware across the Internet

• Stealing the personal information of the infected host, and using the processing power of the botnet to attack networks and create even more identity theft victims

• Using the processing power of botnets to attack the server of a website via millions of "requests" sent at the same time, essentially overloading the server with too much traffic, creating a Denial of Service (DoS) attack.

Why Your Personal Data Is at Risk

According to its latest State of the Net survey, identity theft is soaring. Almost 16 million households have become the victims of identity theft over the past year, up almost 50 percent we project, based on our nationally representative survey of 2,000 respondents.

Almost half of the victims, the magazine added, were notified that their personal information was hacked or lost by a company, government agency, or some other organization. "That's more than double our projection a year ago."

According to the survey, 7.4 million households reported an unauthorized charge on a credit card account.

According to the Secret Service, annual losses associated with credit card fraud are in the billions of dollars. The Secret Service in March thwarted a crime ring in nine states, arresting 19 individuals. "This was an investigation into transnational organized crime, which operated on multiple cyber platforms and whose members bought and sold stolen personal and financial information through online forums," the press release explained. "The group then engaged in crimes such as identity theft and counterfeit credit card trafficking or PIN cashing."

What does PIN cashing mean?

PIN cashing is the fraudulent use of a credit card in order to have access to a banking account and its contents. It is a sort of identity theft, because the unauthorized user will use your personal information in order to have access to your financial resources. This involves using stolen or RFID scanned credit card or debit card information to directly withdraw cash from an identity theft victim's credit line, credit card or bank account. These unauthorized persons get hold of the necessary banking information, and then use it to "cash-in" amounts with the help of automated teller machines (ATMs). *(See page 167)*

Pin cashing is unfortunately a growing phenomenon within the US, where each year the number of fraud victims is significantly growing. The first safety measure one has to undertake is to keep his own banking information secure by reducing the number of online transactions which is the number one responsible for this type of fraud. But if, still online transactions cannot be reduced, always make sure the source is trustworthy and secured.

Take data breach notifications seriously:

Find a credit monitoring service that monitors your credit report on a daily basis and notifies you via email if a significant change is detected. Credit monitoring is one of the best safeguards against identity theft and fraud. In addition, complete Legal access is necessary.

Chapter 9

Social Media Risk
Beware what you Share

Social media is coming of age. Since the emergence of the first social media networks some two decades ago, social media has continued to evolve and offer consumers around the world new and meaningful ways to engage with the people, events and brands that matter to them. Now, years later, social media is still growing rapidly, becoming an integral part of our daily lives. Social networking is now truly a global phenomenon.

People are becoming wiser about how they share their credit-card information and not giving key information, such as Social Security numbers or mothers' maiden names, out over the phone to protect their identities. However, those wishing to steal personal information for their own selfish reasons are now using cellphones and social media to gain access to personal information they can use to access bank accounts, loans, etc.

Because you must divulge some level of personal information in order to use and fully benefit from social networking sites, the risk of identity theft exists for people who use them. Below are some of the ways that you might put yourself at risk of identity theft:

- Using low privacy or no privacy settings
- Accepting invitations to connect from unfamiliar persons or contacts
- Downloading free applications for use on your profile
- Giving your password or other account details to people you know
- Participating in quizzes which may require you to divulge a lot of personal information

- Clicking on links that lead you to other websites, even if the link was sent to you by a friend or posted on your friend's profile
- Falling for email scams (phishing) that ask you to update your social networking profiles
- Using no or out-of-date security software to prevent malicious software from being loaded onto your computer and stealing personal information

Whether purposefully or accidentally, many of us share a staggering amount of private information on the Internet. It is important that individuals and organizations understand the type of information they may be unintentionally sharing.

Protect Yourself:
There are several things you can do to protect your information being accessed:

- Use the least amount of information necessary to register for and use the site. Although this is not possible with all social networking sites, it is best to use a nick-name or handle.
- Create a strong password and change it often. Use a mix of upper and lower case letters, numbers, and characters that are not connected to your personal information (such as birthdates, addresses, last names, etc.).
- Use the highest level privacy settings that the site allows. Do not accept default settings.
- Be wise about what you post. Do not announce when you will be leaving town. Other things you should never post publicly: your address, phone number, driver's license number, social security number (SSN) or student ID number. Only connect to people you already know and trust. Don't put too much out there – even those you know could use your information in a way you didn't intend.
- Read privacy and security policies closely – know what you're getting into. Some major social networking sites actually say they will use or sell information about you in order to display advertising or other information they believe might be useful to you.

- Verify emails and links in emails you supposedly get from your social networking site. These are often designed to gain access to your user name, password, and ultimately your personal information.
- Install a firewall, reputable anti-spam and anti-virus software to protect your information-- and keep it updated!
- Be certain of both the source and content of each file you download. Don't download an executable program just to "check it out." If it's malicious software, the first time you run it, you're system is already infected. In other words, you need to be sure that you trust not only the person or file server that gave you the file, but also the contents of the file itself.
- Beware of hidden file extensions. Windows by default hides the last name extension of a file, so that an innocuous-looking picture file, such as "susie.jpg," might really be "susie.jpg.exe," an executable Trojan or other malicious software. To avoid being tricked, unhide those pesky extensions, so you can see them.
- Use common sense. When in doubt, don't open it, download it, add it, or give information you may have doubts about sharing.

Remember: *The Internet never forgets.*

Beware of Social Media Disasters That Could Strike Your Business

There are at least 14 ways that small businesses could become ensnared by social networking. How many can you name? Knowing what all of these nightmares are means knowing how to prevent them. Ignorance isn't bliss — it's misery. The first step in protecting your organization is to make your employees, executives and members aware at a personal level of the risks of information theft. If they don't understand the value of their own personal data, how will they ever recognize the value of the personal data they handle every day at work?

1. Online reputation integrity.

Do you keep tabs on your company's Facebook page to see just what goes on it? What's being put there by employees? Even "good-natured" things can be taken the wrong way by visitors.

2. Racy text or images

If your employees do this, it could taint your company's reputation. Though you can't control what your teenage employees do on social media at their homes, you *can* educate them. Usually it's ignorance that rules, not malicious intent. Adults too, should be educated that inappropriate posting can tarnish your reputation. This includes something as seemingly innocent as posing half naked on a car in your business's parking lot.

3. Imposters posing as your company

Though it requires some work, it's worth it. Continuously patrol the web to spot any malicious use of your business's name or logo. This includes a phony site purporting to be that of your business. Sign up for Google Alerts so that whenever your business's name appears in a new article or post online, the link gets sent to your email. Of course, just to play safe, don't click on the link inside the email. Instead, copy and paste it into your address box.

4. Financial ID theft

Something as seemingly harmless as posting your employee's new puppy's name could lead to financial identity theft. It's not uncommon for people to use their pet's name as part of a password or answer to a security question. The numbers in birthdays and wedding dates are also commonly used in passwords. Your company's Facebook page should be void of these personal details that a hacker could use to crack passwords. A photo of the puppy is fine, but leave the name a mystery.

5. Geo tracking on photos

Make sure that GPS technology is turned off so that criminals can't stalk you or your employees. Though location-based GPS technology can be a life saver, don't have this turned on unless your life might depend on it.

6. Home robberies

You and your employees should be educated about the dangers of posting vacation or business travel information on social media. Burglars scan these to see whose houses they can rob while the occupants are away on a trip.

7. Corporate snooping

A spy could set up a Facebook page, pose as a fellow employee from another branch and recruit authentic employees to join his Facebook group. This way he can extract sensitive company information over time.

8. Sex offenders

Know whom you connect with online. Tell your employees to use discretion when communicating with a new contact. The new contact could be a sex offender posing as someone innocent.

9. Badmouthing

Sooner or later you may have a disgruntled employee. Maybe it's someone you fired for poor performance. Maybe it's someone still working for you. It could even be your secretary. Do you treat your employees well?

A "picked-on" employee can get revenge by posting bad reviews about your company on various sites, using just their initials or a common name such as "Susan Campbell." This slighted employee may even set up a blog all about how bad your business is. Treat your employees well, and be on the lookout for angry tweets and posts.

10. Bullying

It has happened: an employee posts bully-like comments on the company's Facebook page in response to posts from the public.

11. Government spying

An Associated Press report states "U.S. law enforcement agents are following the rest of the Internet world into popular social-networking services, going undercover with false online profiles to communicate with suspects. Just don't be a 'suspect.'" Don't blindly friend people on Facebook.

12. Phony sites

A criminal or even your business's competition could set up a phony site, maybe on Facebook or a blog-like site, to extract information about your company from unsuspecting visitors or people who've been lured there. This information can include the names of your clients and their emails, phone numbers, account numbers, etc.

13. Account takeover

Earlier this year, the Dow plunged 150 points. Why? The Twitter account for the Associated Press was hacked. The hacker tweeted that President Obama had been injured in a White House attack. Seemingly coming from the AP, this news came across as authentic. Any shocking news tweets that comes from even seemingly legitimate sources should be first carefully considered, as employees may receive these on their Twitter accounts.

14. Legal liability

Though the privacy settings on Facebook can hide posts, this doesn't mean they can't be used as evidence in court.

The bottom line is there's really no such thing as full privacy just because you have the privacy settings switched on. Skilled hackers can penetrate Facebook and dig up the worms.

Chapter 10

File Sharing and
Peer-to-Peer (P2P) Software Safety

One of the great things about the internet is that you can now share files with people all around the globe. Programs like FrostWire, BearShare, Limewire, Morpheus, Kazaa, etc. allow you to share and download movies, music, pictures, almost anything you could want with the online community.

Unfortunately, these programs are not 100% safe. These programs allow users to gain access to your computer and the files that are on it. Not just the files that are in your designated "to share" folder, but potentially everything you have stored on your computer. Users of file share programs have been able to access private pictures, tax return information, banking records, student loan applications, and just about everything else that a person would store on their computer.

Protect Yourself:

There are several things you can do to protect your information being accessed:

- Do not store this kind of information on the same computer you use for file sharing. Have a separate computer set aside specifically for file sharing or store your sensitive information someplace other than on your computer (burned CDs, burned DVDs, external hard drive, etc.)

- Check the security preferences for the program you are using. See if you can set it so that only designated folders can be accessed by the file sharing program.

- Look into encrypting personal and vital information. Some newer computers come with this function already built in. For older computers, there are several companies that offer user-friendly encryption software for your home computer.

Chapter 11

Laptop / Tablet Security

Today's all-in-one spyware suites allow remote monitoring and control on your PC, including access to your keystrokes and webcam. If your system is running suspiciously – the webcam light turns on by itself, apps suddenly start working extra slowly – take a look at your running processes using Windows Task Manager or Activity Monitor on OS X. If you encounter any odd – looking programs hogging system resources, look them up on Google. If you find anything with a bad rep, delete it. If the problem doesn't go away, reinstall your operating system.

The Dos

Treat your laptop like cash.
If you had a wad of money sitting out in a public place, would you turn your back on it — even for just a minute? Would you put it in checked luggage? Leave it on the backseat of your car? Of course not. Keep the same watchful eye on your laptop as you would on your cash.

Lock your laptop with a security cable.
In the office, a hotel, or some other public place, use a laptop security cable. Attach it to something immovable or to a heavy piece of furniture — say, a table or a desk.

Be on guard in airports and hotels.
Keep your eye on your laptop as you go through airport security. Hold onto it until the person in front of you has gone through the metal detector — and keep an eye out when it emerges on the other side. The confusion and shuffle of security checkpoints can be fertile ground for theft.

If you stay in hotels, a security cable may not be enough. Store your laptop in the safe in your room. If you leave your laptop attached to a security cable in your hotel room, consider hanging the "do not disturb" sign on your door.

Consider an alarm.
Depending on your security needs, an alarm on your laptop can be a useful tool. Some laptop alarms sound when there's unexpected motion, or when the computer moves outside a specified range. A program that reports the location of your stolen laptop once it's connected to the internet also can be useful.

Consider carrying your laptop in something else less obvious than a laptop case.
When you take your laptop on the road, carrying it in a computer case may advertise what's inside. Consider using a suitcase, a padded briefcase, or a backpack instead.

The Don'ts
Don't leave it — even for just a minute.
Your conference colleagues seem trustworthy, so you're comfortable leaving your laptop while you network during a break. The people at the coffee shop seem nice, so you ask them to keep an eye on it while you use the restroom. This is not a good idea. Don't leave your laptop unguarded — even for a minute. Take it with you if you can, or at least use a cable to secure it to something heavy.

Don't leave your laptop in a car.
Parked cars are a favorite target of laptop thieves. If you have no choice and you must leave it in your car, keep it locked up and out of sight.

Don't put your laptop on the floor.
No matter where you are in public — at a conference, a coffee shop, or a registration desk — don't put your laptop on the floor. If you must put it down, place it between your feet or up against your leg so you remember that it's there.

Don't keep passwords with your laptop or in its case.
Remembering strong passwords or access numbers can be a challenge. However, leaving them in your laptop carrying case or on your laptop is like leaving your keys in your car. Don't make it easy for a thief to get to your personal or corporate information.

Where to Report a Stolen Laptop
If your laptop is stolen, report it immediately to the local authorities.

- If it's your personal laptop and your information might be misused by an identity thief, visit ftc.gov/idtheft.
- If it's a business laptop, immediately notify your employer, as well. You may want to review the FTC's information about data breaches.

Chapter 12

Smartphone Privacy and Security

Smartphones are the next wave of data hijacking

The increasing use of smartphones for daily activities, such as emailing, banking, web browsing, shopping, bill tracking, social networking, file storage, and entertainment gives your mobile device the ability to know everything about you. Not only do you know your smartphone, but your smartphone knows you. Your smartphone's knowledge, if not protected, is a potential risk to your security and privacy. The ultimate question to ask: Is my privacy and security at risk?

Malware is a rising threat to privacy and security. What is mobile malware? Mobile malware is a program especially created to wreak havoc on your phone. Once installed on your device, it may disrupt the phone's system, in order to gather information stored in the device. It may also gain access to the device's operating system, and take over the phone.

Mobile malware may present itself through fake mobile applications, web-browsing, and SMS/Text messages. There's a gold mine behind that touch screen. Users may not realize how exposed their data is (I dare say most *don't* use password-protection or remote data wiping in case of loss), but criminals know the weak spots, and they're making mobile exploits a high priority

One scenario to watch for: a malicious programmer sneaks a malware-bearing app past smartphone gatekeepers and millions of users realize the honeymoon is over.

Smartphones now track user behavior and location natively and thru third party apps. To find out which apps are accessing personal data on Apple iOS devices, check the privacy settings menu. You can also limit targeted advertising and stop Apple from collecting usage data in the About menu under General settings. On Android devices, find and delete info-sniffing apps from the Application Manager.

- **App-based malware attacks**: may target a user's financial information. This might include bank account numbers, passwords, and PINs. The access of such information may result in the loss of money and/or account take-over.
- **Web-based smartphone attacks**: may result by clicking on an unsafe link. This may potentially give rise to "Phishing" scams or downloading infected files.
- **SMS/Text message-based attacks:** can also be used to spread malware through unsolicited SMS/texts that request the user to reply or click on a link. Unknown to the user, malware may be installed to the device, leading to unauthorized access to the device's information.

Securing your Smartphone device:

- Password-protect your phone. This is the simplest step you can take to prevent your information from being accessed. Make sure it is a strong password that is not similar to or associated with any other personal information.
- Install Security Software. There are a number of companies which offer anti-virus, malware and security software designed especially for smartphones. Make sure to download security software updates.
- Be aware of what you are doing on your phone. The same precautions you would take while on your home computer apply to your smartphone. Double check URLs for accuracy, don't open suspicious links, and make sure a site is secure (https) before giving any billing or personal information.
- Do not "jail-break" or use a "jail-broken" phone. A "jail-broken" phone is a phone that has gone through a process which opens

its operating system to applications which would otherwise not be compatible with the operating system. However, once "jail-broken," the phone is vulnerable to anything the user downloads. Note: The application necessary to jail-break an iPhone may put both your phone and PC at risk.

- When installing an app on any smartphone, take the time to read the "small print." Evaluate the information the app requires access to, and consider if this information is necessary for the app to run successfully. If you cannot see a reason for the app to have access to the information, you should reconsider installing the app.

- Install a "phone finder" app. These apps are designed to help you find your phone if it becomes lost or stolen.

- Enroll in a backup / wiping program. You can enroll in a program that will back up the information on your smartphone to your home computer. Many of these services are also able to remotely "wipe" your phone if it is lost or stolen so that no data remains on the device itself. These services are available through your smartphone's manufacturer or through your wireless provider.

- Limit your activities while using public Wi-Fi. Try not to purchase things or access email while using a public Wi-Fi zone. Public Wi-Fi hotspots are targeted by hackers since they can give the hacker direct access to your mobile device. Using your 3G or 4G network provider connection is much more secure than using a public Wi-Fi connection.

- Check URLs before making a purchase using your smartphone. Any page that requires credit card information should start with https://. This means it is a secured site.

Note: Do not allow your device to remember passwords. If your device is lost or stolen, the information is now compromised.

Android, iPhone, or BlackBerry: Which one do you have?

- Regardless of whether you are an Android user, an iPhone user, or even a Blackberry user, your privacy and security may be at risk. Understanding the operating system of your Smartphone will require work on your part. This knowledge will help you understand the capabilities of your device and help you understand the threat to privacy and security.

- All three platforms have their own App Stores and all three employ different security measures to monitor and vet the apps that are allowed to be on the Android Market, the Apple App Store, or the Blackberry App Store:
  - o **Android's Google Market** runs an open market. As the Smartphone industry grows, it attracts more malware developers to organize attacks and put Smartphone privacy and security at risk. The Android Market has been criticized by the industry several times for not vetting its mobile applications before they are added to the Android Market. What does this mean for you Android phone users? You will need to exercise caution when downloading apps to your device.
  - o If you are an **iPhone** user, Apple reviews applications before they are added to the App Store. According to *Computerworld*, "When Apple reviews an app, it tries to verify several things, including these: Does the app do what it says it does? Does it function reliably? And does it respect the limitations that Apple has put on developers?" However, despite tighter security measures, it does not exempt the iPhone user from privacy and security threats.
  - o The **BlackBerry** Smartphone is trying to make a comeback and, despite being marginally behind the leading Apple and Android phones, its designer, Research in Motion (RIM) designed the phone with security in mind – encrypting data and giving its users the ability to control "how mobile applications interact with a BlackBerry and all of the data stored on it" – according to *Computerworld*.

Application Permissions/Access:

Ever wonder if the apps that you download put you at risk? If not, you probably should. Many apps are designed to capture a wide range of information. Did you know that apps can:

- Read phone state and identity?
- Track your location?
- Read owner data?
- Read contact data?
- Record audio – your calls?
- Take pictures?
- Modify or delete SD card content?
- Edit SMS/text or MMS messages?
- Write sync settings?
- Send SMS messages?
- Write contact data?
- Full internet access?

The best security practices when downloading apps are exercising caution and reviewing the app's ratings, regardless of whether the app is free or paid.

You should carefully examine and pay attention to the permissions the app is requesting to access:

- Android Market apps require the user to either grant or deny access – if you deny access you will not be able to download and install the app.
- BlackBerry devices allow the user to go back to application permissions to modify or remove the 'Trusted Application' status. The status gives the application permission to access sensitive functionality on the device, which includes phone, GPS, and Internet – once given trusted permission, the application will not prompt the user for permission again before accessing the phone's data.
- iPhone apps will not disclose what the application has permission to access. When downloading an app whether free or paid, Apple requires the recognition of consent by having

the user sign in using their Apple account. The primary reason behind Apple's non-disclosure of the information, according to *Computerworld*, is because "Apple tries to prevent developers from having full-scale access to all of the data and hardware" on a device running on Apple's operating system. However, apps still have access to certain system components.

Because apps have access to a lot of your personal information and data on your Smartphone, exercise a great level of caution when downloading apps and familiarize yourself with what the app really needs in order to run. If you feel it requires more than it really should, reconsider installing it.

Only download applications you trust. Android users are allowed to download apps from third-parties, whereas, iPhone users are only allowed to download apps from the Apple Store; unless, of course the iPhone has been "jail-broken." Jail-broken iPhones can download applications from the "Cydia App Store" (apps that have not been approved by Apple).

Location (GPS) and WiFi:

- Many applications request permission to access location. Consider turning off the location services (GPS) on your phone to protect your location privacy, unless it is necessary to perform a desired function. Keep in mind that you have the ability to enable and disable the location services on your phone.
- Have you ever taken photographs with your Smartphone and posted them online? What's the worst that can happen? As careful as you may be, if your GPS is enabled, your personal information may be exposed through a process called "geotagging."
  - According to *Wikipedia*, "Geotagging is the process of adding geographical identification 'metadata' to various media such as photographs, video, websites,

SMS messages, or RSS feeds and is a form of geospatial metadata."

- o This information most often includes latitude and longitude coordinates which are derives from a global positioning system (GPS).
- o While it sounds complicated, it really isn't. It simply means the marking of a video, photo, or other media with an embedded location of where it was taken.
- o Smartphones featuring GPS have made this "tagging" possible.
- o "Geotagging" has been considered an infringement on public privacy and problems can arise if the information is given out unknowingly and/ or pulled by the wrong people. So, the photograph you took in front of your computer, at your doorstep, etc. has been recorded and may have possibly given your location.
- • To protect yourself, you can:
- o Turn the geotagging feature off.
- o Download disabling software (it will search for geotagging information and delete it before sending).
- o Be aware and educate yourself. Understand the information you are sharing.
- o Consider what you post on the Internet. You never know who has access to it.
- • Protect your privacy and security by exercising caution while doing financial transactions or checking banking information while connected to public wireless networks (WiFi). Credit card and personal information transmitted through public WiFi may be up for grabs by identity thieves.
- • If you are a Smartphone user, it is highly recommended to use your Provider's 4/5G Network to conduct any financial business. After all, you are paying for the service.

Chapter 13

License Plate Tracking

Services such as MVTrac and Vigilant Solutions maintain nationwide databases of car location info for law enforcement agencies and repo agents. If you're not the original owner of your vehicle, make sure its past doesn't come back to haunt you in the form of a surprise towing or false arrest-check the National Insurance Crime Bureau database to see if your car or truck has ever been reported stolen, and check with local law enforcement to see if a creditor has marked it for repossession.

Chapter 14

One Good Deed Could Lead to Identity Theft

In light of recent natural disasters, relief efforts often spring up overnight, making it difficult for the person who genuinely wants to contribute to recognize the difference between real charity efforts and fraudulent ones. Fraudsters are increasingly adept at making a scam charity seem legitimate; therefore, even in times of tragedy, individuals must use caution, rather than emotion, when providing assistance.

The Federal Bureau of Investigation (FBI) and the National Center for Disaster Fraud have issued the following guidelines to help donors avoid becoming victims of a charity scam:

Do not respond to unsolicited (spam) incoming emails, including clicking links contained within those messages.

Be skeptical of individuals representing themselves as surviving victims or officials asking for donations via email or social networking sites.

Beware of organizations with copy-cat names similar to but not exactly the same as those of reputable charities.

Rather than following a purported link to a website, verify the legitimacy of non-profit organizations by utilizing various Internet-based resources that may assist in confirming the group's existence and its non-profit status.

Chapter 15

An Alert Concerning Charitable Donations

Be cautious of emails that claim to show pictures of the disaster areas in attached files because the files may contain viruses. Only open attachments from known senders. ..

To ensure contributions are received and used for intended purposes, make contributions directly to known organizations rather than relying on others to make the donation on your behalf.

Do not be pressured into making contributions, as reputable charities do not use such tactics.

Do not give your personal or financial information to anyone who solicits contributions. Providing such information may compromise your identity and make you vulnerable to identity theft.

Avoid cash donations if possible. Pay by debit or credit card, or write a check directly to the charity. Do not make checks payable to individuals.

Chapter 16

Emergency Situations

Hurricanes, tornados, fires, earthquakes and man-made disasters are frightening and cause a lot of chaos. Taking the time today to create an action plan might help you avoid future identity theft related situations.

Be prepared to evacuate. Keep photocopies of these items readily available, preferably in a sealed large envelope or a locked box.

- Birth certificates for each family member
- A current photograph of each family member
- Driver's licenses
- Social Security cards for each family member
- Death certificates
- Insurance papers, wills, deeds, property records, and photos or video of personal belongings
- Other vital papers for each family member, such as immigration papers, marriage licenses
- Financial account information that might be needed in an emergency
- Brief medical histories including medical equipment/supply need including style/serial numbers, all prescriptions and dosages for each family member.
- Medical insurance cards.

Evacuation:

- Place the box or sealed envelope in your car only when you are ready to leave. Be aware that thieves sometimes loot cars parked in driveways of those who are evacuating. You will need those papers to identify yourself with various assistance groups and with insurance companies.

- Keep the locked box (or envelope) in sight at all times, even in a shelter. If necessary, remove these papers from the locked box and put them in a large plastic bag taped to your inner clothing. Don't trust anyone, other than family members, to watch these documents.

- Few people want to leave computers behind. If you are time-crunched or limited in space, remove the hard-drive and take that with you. It can always be put in a new computer. Many people are using "USB backup drives" for regular backups of critical information. These can be removed in a few seconds during an emergency. You may also want to carry an extra pair of glasses with you.

Avoid Scams:

- "Phishing Scams": Con artists pretend to call from a company that "lost data." They will ask for bank account, credit card or Social Security numbers. This is always a scam. Companies will not contact you this way.

- Relief Group Solicitations: Scam artists may pretend to be calling on behalf of a relief agency trying to raise donations. During a time of crisis, legitimate relief agencies are too busy attending to the immediate needs of victims. Only donate if you initiate the call to a well-established group. Hang up on any telephone solicitors asking for donations.

In most emergency situations, the media will be a primary source of information alerting you on actions to take and scams to avoid.

Chapter 17

Medicare Cards and Social Security Numbers

Many consumers complain that while they remove their Social Security cards from their wallets, the Social Security Number is still on their Medicare cards.

I would like to make the following recommendation. Not only could this tip keep an identity thief from getting your number, but it may also save your life one day.

- Photocopy your Medicare card, front and back.
- Put your original card in a safe, locked area. Only carry it with you on the days you KNOW you will need it.
- Using scissors cut the photocopies of your Medicare card down to wallet size, cutting off the last four (4) numbers of your Social Security Number.
- Staple these two business card size papers together, adding a third blank paper to the packet. On this blank sheet, write down following:

  o Emergency contact with the name and phone number of a person who can be reached in the event of an emergency. Your emergency contact person should have a sheet of paper with the last 4 numbers of your Social Security number and the following:
    - Your pertinent medical history
    - The name of your doctors
    - A list of all the prescriptions you take, including over-the-counter pills.

Put a PIN on your SSN.

Did you know you can lock down your Social Security Number to prevent thieves from filing your taxes early? It won't help other forms of ID theft, but it stops this. Attached is a link to the form you would need to submit this IRS form -_www.irs.gov/pub/irs-pdf/f14039.pdf

But shouldn't the IRS be watching for "any questionable activity" on accounts anyway? Every taxpayer and business entity is a potential victim of ID theft and tax fraud. Consumers need to file early, be diligent about accounts, and take responsibility to protect their own information.

You are absolutely right, but they don't do a very good job of that. Google "IRS tax refund fraud" or that ilk, and you'll see that this is a growing problem for the IRS. And while tax refund fraud is bad, the theft of your SSN can be devastating, since it can be used to create bogus accounts and synthetic IDs. Financial fraud is only one area of concern from SSN theft, and is the easiest to detect and easiest to correct (not "easy", just "easiest"); worse is medical or criminal use from manufactured IDs.

I recently spoke with a group of folks in South Carolina about this, because the South Carolina Department of Revenue had over 6.4 million tax records stolen in September, 2012. Those folks will likely be fighting for their identities for years.

And I agree with you that everyone should be diligent and responsible to protect their own information, but with breaches of companies, hospitals, schools, and government agencies rampant these days, the security of your identity is beyond your ability to adequately manage, in my opinion.

Chapter 18

Medical Identity Theft

Medical identity theft is a rapidly growing and frightening issue that now impacts almost 6% of Americans. A recent study by the Ponermon Institute and The National Study on Medical Identity Theft indicates there have been more than 4 million victims of medical identity theft in the last two years alone. Half of medical identity theft victims know the person who stole their IDs, and victims end up footing the bills in many cases. Medical identity theft has more than doubled since 2008 – with no end in sight.

Medical identity theft results from the fraudulent use of an individual's personal information, Social Security number, or health insurance information to obtain medical goods and services, money through insurance fraud, or insurance coverage for treatments. This may result in a number of problems for the victim which might include a collection account for a past due bill, medical insurance filing errors, or distorted medical records that could affect future medical treatment. It typically takes a victim almost two years to resolve the fraudulent charges.

One truly disturbing aspect of medical identity theft is just how easy it is to commit. Thieves can obtain your information through lost or stolen purses and wallets, written correspondence found in your mailbox, breaches in data security, unscrupulous medical personnel, or even family members and colleagues who have access to your information. In fact, it's reported that 50% of medical ID theft occurred when a friend or family member used an individual's medical information without their knowledge. Even more troubling is that because medical ID theft requires less information than traditional identity fraud (often no SSN is required when seeking services), anyone with a medical history can be at risk.

The reasons for these complications are mainly attributed to the lack of a central repository of medical history and the extensive privacy laws in relation to medical file disclosure. It is difficult to discover and the fraud may exist until uncovered through a myriad of methods.

A bad sign in all of this: Most people never check their medical records for fraud.

Medical Privacy in the Electronic Age: Personal Health Records and Your Privacy

Today you have more reason than ever to care about the privacy of your medical information. Intimate details you revealed in confidence to your doctor were once stored in locked file cabinets and on dusty shelves in the medical records department. Healthcare accountted for one of the largest groups of identities stolen in 2014.

Now, sensitive information about your physical and mental health will almost certainly end up in data files. Your records may be seen by hundreds of strangers who work in health care, the insurance industry, and a host of businesses associated with medical organizations. What's worse, your private medical information is now a valuable commodity for marketers who want to sell you something.

If you established care with a medical office tomorrow, would you be able to give your new doctor a complete copy of your medical records, lab tests and a list of your prescription drugs? If you're like most Americans, your health information is split among your various health care providers. For example, you may have records at a hospital, a physician's office, your dentist, a pharmacy, and an optician's dispensary.

Since each health care provider maintains its own file on you, it can be challenging to get control of your medical records. However, HIPAA's right to access coupled with the emerging market for the Personal Health Record (PHR) is changing that.

You have a right to access your medical records.

Under the Health Insurance Portability and Accountability Act (HIPAA), the federal medical privacy law, you have a right to obtain copies of the medical records maintained by your health care providers. This means you can gather information from multiple sources and keep your medical history as a single record.

A PHR allows you to keep your own record of your medical history, and is usually an electronic system or software that provides a centralized storage space for your health information. A PHR may also support options such as secure email with your physicians and links to medical informational websites and archives.

PHRs have the potential to help individuals become better informed about their medical history and more engaged in their own healthcare. However, as with all types of electronic records, PHRs do present certain privacy and security concerns.

Many PHRs are not covered under HIPAA.

A key question when considering the use of a PHR is whether it is covered by HIPAA. Only PHRs offered by a "covered entity" are subject to HIPAA. Covered entities include health care providers, health plans and health care clearinghouses. All other PHRs are not subject to HIPAA. While some commercial PHRs may advertise themselves as "HIPAA-compliant," the only privacy protections they offer are those in their own privacy notices and policies, which they can change at any time.

PHRs for Californians *may* be covered by the Confidentiality of Medical Information Act (CMIA), depending upon the interpretation of California law. Until the law is tested in court, it may not be completely clear whether PHR vendors are subject to the CMIA's information privacy requirements.

Consider privacy and security when choosing a PHR.

The risk that data will be lost or stolen is inherent to data stored in an electronic format. Hackers are becoming increasingly sophisticated and medical identity theft is a rising problem.

While the PHR's security may be somewhat beyond your control, you should be notified if your data has been breached – under both federal and California law.

HIPAA-covered PHRs have more stringent security and privacy requirements. Until stronger protections are in place for *all* PHRs, we recommend choosing a HIPAA-covered PHR; however they may limit your ability to centralize records from multiple health providers.

If you are considering using a commercial PHR, read its "notice of privacy practices" and privacy policy first. A notice of privacy practices applies specifically to the PHR product and the information collected in it; a privacy policy explains the company's overall privacy and security policies.

The following are some questions you should keep in mind when reading a PHR's privacy notice and policy:

How will your information's security be safeguarded? Will it be encrypted when it is stored and transmitted? Does the vendor store your medical information in the cloud and how secure is that storage?

Is the PHR data stored in the U.S.? If it is not, it will not be protected by any U.S. laws.

What does the vendor say about how it may use or disclose your information? Does it mention disclosure of de-identified or aggregate data (an indication that it is selling the data)?

Who will have access to your medical information? What control do you have over access to the information in your PHR? Will your information be sold to or shared with third parties, such as marketers? Can you find out who accessed your medical information?

Can you cancel the PHR? What happens to the medical information that is in the PHR if you do cancel? Does the vendor keep the data and continue sharing it or does the vendor destroy all the data that is in your PHR?

How does the PHR generate revenue? Keep in mind that they are businesses and that monetizing your medical information may be part of their business plan.

Do you have any ability to delete information that has already been sent to providers from the PHR?
What support does the vendor offer for the PHR? How do you contact customer service and what is the response time?

Not comfortable with electronic PHRs? You can still accomplish the same goal by consolidating printouts or paper copies of your medical records and keeping them in a secure place.

Discovery: Ways an individual might discover medical identity theft

Some of the ways victims discovered their personal information was used by another person for medical purposes include: Receipt of an Explanation of Benefits statement from your health insurer listing services or treatments that were never provided. Receipt of a bill for services or equipment that were never provided. Collection account listed on a credit report that is the result of an unpaid medical bill not related to any valid services provided. Denial of health insurance or notice of increase in premiums based on a medical condition that you do not have. Inaccuracy found in medical record held by physician or hospital. Alert received from a healthcare provider, law enforcement agency, or an insurance company who has discovered the fraud.

Am I at Risk for Medical ID Theft?

One truly disturbing aspect of medical ID theft is just how easy it is to commit. Thieves can obtain your information through lost or stolen purses and wallets, written correspondence found in your mailbox, breaches in data security, unscrupulous medical personnel, or even family members and colleagues who have access to your information. In fact, it's reported that 33% of medical ID theft occurred when a friend or family member used an individual's medical information without their knowledge. Even more troubling is that because medical ID theft requires less information than traditional identity fraud (often no SSN is required when seeking services), anyone with a medical history can be at risk.

Proactive steps: Early detection of medical identity theft

These steps may help detect signs of medical identity theft early and are instrumental in limiting the amount of damage done by an identity thief. Review your health insurance provider's Explanation of Benefits statement for any activity that is not correct. Obtain your "benefits request" each year from your insurance provider. This is a listing of benefits paid in your name by your health insurer. If you do not recognize any payments, follow up with the insurer or provider to learn more.

What can happen if my identity is stolen?

With costs averaging more than $20,000 to resolve cases of medical ID theft, a potentially huge financial burden is only one of the repercussions victims may face. These costs can include billing for services or treatments you didn't receive, higher premiums, or even outright loss of health insurance. To say nothing of the time and distress correcting the theft will cause or the potential credit issues resulting from erroneous billing.

But financial problems aren't the only danger. In fact, given the nature of this crime, monetary complications very well may be the least of your problems. Consider a scenario where you find yourself in a hospital seeking care. If your medical ID is stolen you may discover your health benefits completely depleted. Even more dangerous is the possibility of additional or inaccurate information and data in your medical records – the very same records physicians and other medical personnel will reference to treat you. An inaccurate blood type or noted allergy could quickly escalate an emergency room visit into a life-threatening situation or worse.

Important Information

Request your medical records if you have any suspicion of fraud. You have the right to request copies of records from any entity covered by the Health Insurance Portability and Accountability Act of 1996 (HIPAA) that maintains information or is suspected to have information about you. These organizations are subject to the HIPAA privacy rules and have an obligation to provide you with your medical history.

Request an "accounting of disclosure." Under HIPAA, this is a list of any entities that have received personally identifiable healthcare information for uses unrelated to treatment and payment. These reports are available once every 12 months, free of charge. Order your annual Medical Information Bureau (MIB) report by calling 1-866-692-6901. These reports provide information regarding underwritten life, health, or disability income insurance and could indicate fraudulent insurance filings. Not everyone has a file with the MIB. Note that, according to www.mib.com, only 20% of consumers have a record with the Medical Information Bureau. The reports are available once every 12 months, free of charge.

Common types of health insurance fraud

Medical Equipment Fraud: Equipment manufacturers offer "free" products to individuals. Insurers are then charged for products that were not needed and/or may not have been delivered. "Rolling Lab" Schemes: Unnecessary and sometimes fake tests are given to individuals at health clubs, retirement homes, or shopping malls and billed to insurance companies or Medicare.

Services Not Performed: Customers or providers bill insurers for services never rendered by changing bills or submitting fake ones.

Medicare Fraud: Medicare fraud can take the form of any of the health insurance frauds listed previously. Senior citizens are frequent targets of Medicare schemes, especially by medical equipment manufacturers who offer seniors free medical products in exchange for their Medicare numbers. Because a physician has to sign a form certifying that equipment or testing is needed before Medicare pays for it, con artists fake signatures or bribe corrupt doctors to sign the forms. Once a signature is in place, the manufacturers bill Medicare for merchandise or service that was not needed or was not ordered.

Tips for avoiding health insurance fraud

Never sign blank insurance claim forms. Never give a blank authorization to a medical provider to bill for services rendered. Ask your medical providers what they will charge and what you will be expected to pay out-of-pocket.

Do not do business with door-to-door or telephone salespeople who tell you that services or medical equipment are free.

Give your insurance or Medicare identification only to those who have provided you with medical services.

Keep accurate records of all healthcare appointments.

Know if your doctor ordered equipment for you.

-Federal Bureau of Investigation –

The Newest Medical Scam Targets Diabetics

One in four adults is considered pre-diabetic, but few realize the serious health risk they face if there condition turns into diabetes. If not managed properly, diabetes can lead to complications such as blindness, heart disease, kidney failure and amputations.

Handling diabetes can be extremely resource intensive – both on your time and your wallet. So when some diabetics received a call from someone offering free glucose meters, diabetic test strips, lancets and other supplies, it seemed like a blessing. However, they are likely unknowingly talking to a scammer attempting to steal their personal information.

The Department of Health and Human Services, Office of Inspector General (OIG) recently put out a fraud alert (*see below*) warning diabetics about this scam, which has been reported all over the country. In this scam, the thieves will call victims claiming to be a Medicare employee or a member of a legitimate diabetes group. They will offer perks such as free drugs or supplies in exchange for Medicare, financial, or other personal information.

After obtaining the information, the opportunities for the thieves are endless. Some have used Medicare numbers for medical identity theft: obtaining benefits under the victims' name, defrauding the government and the victim. Others have used the Social Security numbers and other information to open credit.

If you receive a call from the government or a health organization asking for your personal information, hang up! Both the government and organizations such as The American Diabetes Association claim they never ask for personal information over the phone. If you have reason to believe the call is legitimate, obtain the callers information, then look up the organizations listed contact information and call them to handle matters.

Fraud Alert for People with Diabetes

Criminals who plot to defraud the Government and steal money from the American people have a new target: people with diabetes.

Although the precise method may vary, the scheme generally involves someone pretending to be from the Government, a diabetes association, or even Medicare, calling you. The caller offers "free" diabetic supplies, such as glucose meters, diabetic test strips, or lancets. The caller may also offer other supplies such as heating pads, lift seats, foot orthotics, or joint braces, in exchange for the beneficiaries' Medicare or financial information, or confirmation of this type of personal information. Additionally, you may receive items in the mail that you did not order.

The call is a scam

If you receive such a call, OIG recommends the following actions:

1. Protect Your Medicare and Other Personal Information

Do not provide your Medicare number or other personal information. Be suspicious of anyone who offers free items or services and then asks for your Medicare or financial information. These calls are not coming from Medicare, diabetes associations, or other similar organizations. While the caller says the items are "free," the items are still billed to Medicare. Once your Medicare information is in the hands of a dishonest person or supplier, you are susceptible to further scams. Alert others about this scheme, and remind them not to provide strangers Medicare numbers or other personal information.

2. Report the Call to Law Enforcement

Report the call to the OIG Hotline at 1-800-HHS-TIPS or online at http://oig.hhs.gov/fraud/report-fraud/. As part of your report, provide the name of the company that called you, the company's telephone number and address, and a summary of your conversation with the caller.

3. Check Your Medicare Summary Notice and Medicare Bills

Check your Medicare Summary Notice and other medical information to see if you were charged for items you did not order or did not receive. Also, check for items that were billed multiple times, such as glucose meters, diabetes test strips and lancets, and other supplies. Report any irregular activity to your health care provider and the OIG Hotline at 1-800-HHS-TIPS or online at http://oig.hhs.gov/fraud/report-fraud/.

4. Do Not Accept Items That You Did Not Order

You are under no obligation to accept items that you did not order. Instead, you should refuse the delivery and/or return to the sender. Keep a record of the sender's name and the date you returned the item(s) to help OIG catch any future illegal billing.

The Department of Health and Human Services, Office of Inspector General (OIG) fights fraud in Government programs. As part of this effort, the OIG relies upon alert citizens to help them catch those who steal from American taxpayers.

Time Out!

Let's stop right here for just a moment and let me share something personal with you.

Why are you reading about diabetes? On Sunday morning, Thanksgiving week-end 2011, I passed out while in church. After three days in the hospital and multiple tests, I was diagnosed with Type ll diabetes and I had gone into diabetic shock. I had not been a patient in the hospital in forty-five years. No one in my family has ever had diabetes. The doctors told me I needed to change my diet, start exercising and get my eyes checked. Then my eye doctor sent me to a Retina Specialist. I was diagnosed with Diabetic Retinopathy and was told I was losing vision in one eye and had a 50/50 chance of total loss in the other, without immediate surgeries.

It's been over three years, I'm 55 lbs. lighter, and my doctors have told me if I continue to eat right and exercise, I will be able to come off all my diabetes related medications soon. After eleven eye surgeries with two awesome surgeons at two different hospitals my vision is starting to stabilize in one eye and I can start driving again.

*Now you know my story and why I had the time to do all the necessary research to write this book. So, if you get nothing else of value from this book, **Get Your Blood Sugar Checked Once A Year,** and tell others to do the same!*

*Our time out is over. So, let's get back to **"Deploy Predator Surveillance."***

Chapter 19

Clearing Criminal Identity Theft

The following are general steps you must take to clear your name of an erroneous criminal record. These procedures are likely to vary somewhat from jurisdiction to jurisdiction.

Working with Law Enforcement Agencies:

- Contact the *arresting law enforcement agency*
    - o Explain this is a case of misidentification and that someone is using your personal information.
    - o Request that the *arresting law enforcement agency* indicate what form/s of identification or biometric data were collected or captured at the time of arrest or citation (fingerprints, mug shot). Get as much detail about the crime as possible. Who, what, where, when. This information will help you to prove your innocence.
- Contact your *local law enforcement agency*.
    - o File a "false personation"/identity theft report.
    - o Ask your *local law enforcement agency* to take prints and verify your identity and forward directly to the *arresting law enforcement agency*. They may want:
        - A full set of your fingerprints
        - Your photograph
        - Any photo identification documents such as a driver's

license, passport, or U.S. legal presence documents.

- o If fingerprints were NOT taken by the *arresting law enforcement agency*; use signature verification and any relative remarks made on the arrest or citation form by the officer, i.e. scars, marks, tattoos, and height and weight.

- Request that the *arresting law enforcement agency* compare the prints and/or photographs to establish your innocence, once your identity has been established, the *arresting law enforcement agency* should recall any warrants and issue a "clearance letter" or certificate of release (if you were arrested/booked) which you will need to keep in your possession at all times.

- Request that the *arresting law enforcement agency* file with the district attorney's office and/or court of jurisdiction the follow-up investigation.

- Request that the *arresting law enforcement agency* change all records from your name to the imposter's true identity or to John Doe if unknown.

- Request the *arresting law enforcement agency* forward a clearance update to the levels of databases that must be cleared include city, county, state, and federal data bases.

Note: Due to authentication issues, most law enforcement agencies will only accept this information in person, or by submission from another law enforcement agency.

Working with the Court:
You will need to determine the specific law(s) in your state that enable you to clear your name in the court records. A judge or magistrate will be required to make this determination.

From the court you will need to request:

- A declaration that you are factually innocent of charges based upon the follow-up impersonation investigation by the law enforcement agency, or declarations, affidavits, or other material and relevant information.
- This action will change the name on the arrest records and the warrant of arrest to that of the imposter (if the true identity of the imposter is known).
- Your name will then be known as an alias of the imposter.
- The court should be requested to provide written verification for you to carry.

DMV:

If tickets or driving records are involved the victim should contact the Department/Bureau of Motor Vehicles:

- Ask to speak to the fraud department or investigator.
- Explain that you are a victim of identity theft
- Ask for the required procedure to prove you are innocent. (perhaps sending letter of clearance from the law enforcement agency)

BAD BACKGROUND CHECKS:

What additional considerations should I be aware of regarding employment?

Follow the steps above then follow up with background check companies individually and with each perspective employer.

Even though you may have cleared up the records with the local, state and federal systems, it is possible for negative information to still pop up on a background report. If this should occur, you must ask the company which background screening company they used. You will then need to show your documentation of clearance to that background screening company in order to clear their records. You probably will also want to provide the clearance documents directly to the employer to help defuse the matter.

This solution should not be used in lieu of legal advice. If you do not have an attorney as a Legal Services Coordinator; I would be glad to make a recommendation. We have access to top quality Law Firms with over 7,900 Attorneys nationwide.

Chapter 20

High Tech Identity Hijacking

Are there RFID chips in your pocket?

Is Big Brother in your grocery cart?

RFID))))))

How often do you go to the store on a monthly basis? Maybe you go down to the local coffee shop every morning before work. This is prime hunting ground for an attacker to steal all of your credit card information without ever touching you, using equipment they got on ebay. These are the threats that the credit card companies and the thieves don't want you to know about.

RFID, Radio Frequency Identification, is the technology that lets you simply wave your credit card, passport or license in front of a nearby scanner instead of having to slide the magnetic stripe through it. Millions of new credit cards and passports contain these tiny two way radios. Visa calls its technology PayWave, MasterCard dubs it PayPass, Discover brands it Zip, and American Express calls it ExpressPay. These tiny tracking devices the size of a grain of dust, can be used to secretly scan you and the things you're carrying – right thru your clothes, wallet, backpack or purse. This makes it easy for thieves to employ electronic pickpocketing and scan your credit card numbers and other info without touching you! It's a fairly simple concept. The electronic scanner sends a signal which is received by an antenna embedded into the card, which is connected to the card's RFID chip, thus activating it.

Confession time: *"I was going to leave RFID Card Calling and Sinking out of this book. The RFID chip in a credit card emits the account number, expiration data and other information. I was not sure if this really could happen. Then to my surprise it happened at a local restaurant in my home town. After this, I did extensive research and found out that this has become one of our latest threats and it could happen to you."*

Server Charged in Credit Card Scam

Tuscaloosa, AL. - Police have charged a former Jim 'N Nicks Bar-B-Que server with stealing credit card information from customers.

Investigators began receiving calls from people who had used their credit cards at the same restaurant. The restaurant's managers worked with police and determined that every victim had the same server.

They determined that the server would swipe a victim's credit or debit card on a skimmer device that would capture card information.

The server gave the device to another man who is accused of putting the card numbers on other cards.

Those cards were used at several different stores.

The restaurant server was charged with trafficking in stolen identities.

Investigators filed court documents alleging the other man charged $3,826 to the cards of the four victims.   — *Tuscaloosa News 11/02/12*

Just like a submarine uses sonar to seek out a ship it's trying to sink, the criminals send a radio signal or "ping" from a standard checkout contactless card reader purchased online for under $500. The victim's credit cards' antennae automatically answer the call by providing their card information. The criminal then uses this card information to make purchases, thereby "sinking the card."

About 200 million credit cards now have this technology embedded into them. However, over the next 2-3 years, it is expected that credit card issuers will replace every single magnetic stripe credit and debit card with a new contactless smartcard, and why shouldn't they? The new cards seem to make it all easier. So much easier that some folks are reading your credit cards before you even take them out of your wallet.

Those folks are called identity thieves, and the unfortunate truth is that RFID technology has made identity theft quite literally a stroll in the park. Where credit card "Skimming" used to require the thief to get his hands on your card, acquiring your personal data is now as easy as passing you on the street.

RFID readers

Readers are employed by convenience stores, pharmacies, restaurants, fast food markets, and many other places of business. Credit card companies say it keeps your identity safer, because your card is never in the hands of a stranger. Readers include safety features to keep your data from being intercepted once it has been read from your card.

However, these same readers can be freely purchased and attached to a laptop or cell phone with very little technical knowledge required. They've even created cell phones with built in card readers that can steal your information. How many times have you walked by someone carrying a tablet computer case? Would you even be suspicious? By simply walking past you, this person acquires your credit card number, expiration date and more to do with what he pleases.

RFID chips are becoming more and more common. How can you keep your identity safe? One way is to be suspicious of every passing pedestrian.

RFID and Other Cards
The use of RFID tagging in identification extends far beyond payment cards. Right now many corporations are using contactless cards to maintain security in their buildings. However, RFID actually poses a huge threat to that security. Hackers can use RFID readers to scan and then copy ID cards. To an electronic reader, ID cards and their clones are seen as identical.

Because of federal mandate HSPD-12, all government agencies are required to switch to a new ID card that uses RFID. This mandate requires all government employees to keep these new ID cards in an RFID blocking sleeve or badge holder for privacy and security. *Shouldn't you protect your privacy the same way? (See page 166)*

All US passports issued since October 2006 also have RFID chips in them. The chip contains all the data that is on the first page including your photo. It has been shown that hackers can determine what country a passport has been issued from without even reading all the data on it, simply by recognizing the way the chip responds to certain scans.

A growing number of states (New York, Michigan, Washington, and Vermont, to name a few) are now issuing special driver's licenses "enhanced" with long range RFID chips. **Enhanced Driver's Licenses** (EDLs) can be scanned from your wallet, while you are still in your car. EDLs make travel across the border a little easier, and if not kept in a shielding privacy sleeve, unwanted invasion of your privacy much more "convenient".

However until recently, the press and major credit card companies have been slow to recognize the privacy dangers associated with RFID chips that have been used in commercial and private sectors. Examples of their use would be in items such as credit cards, debit cards, passports, drivers' licenses, healthcare cards, ID cards, and transportation cards including most subway fare cards.

Part 2

Are your children safe?

Now Identity Thieves are Targeting Children for Unused Social Security Numbers.

Chapter 21

Child Identity Theft Growing Everyday

Identity theft has DOUBLED in the past year for children age 5 and younger

Child identity theft occurs when a child's identity is used by another person for the imposter's personal gain. It is a perennial crime that has taken on new dimensions in the Information Age. The perpetrator may be a family member or someone known by the family. It could also be a stranger who purposely targets children because of the lengthy time between the theft of the information and the discovery of the crime. A 2013 study, by the Washington, D.C.-based Identity Theft Assistance Center, found that child identity theft is even more difficult to detect and resolve than adult identity theft

Some say a child is a blank slate, yet to be written upon. To parents this means a long life of opportunity. Unfortunately it means the same to identity thieves. The epidemic of child identity theft revealed last year is continuing to grow at a rapid pace.

The new data seems to confirm that the younger the child, the more likely they will be a victim of identity theft. That's because this gives the thief more time to go undetected while they use the child's identity. The Federal Trade Commission (FTC), the nation's consumer protection agency, cautions that when children are victims of identity theft, the crime may go undetected for years — or at least until they apply for a job, a student loan or a car loan, or want to rent an apartment.

Over 4 million children have already been victims of identity theft. Of course, this is the number of discovered cases; the actual number may be much higher. It is important to be careful about how and why you share your child's information. Identity theft is a very personal crime, and it can take years to get a child's identity back after it's been stolen.

"I owe $46,000 on my credit cards, my condo is in foreclosure, I've been labeled a thief and I'll be 6 on my next birthday"

Cyber-Centric World

The digital age has brought on a new set of digital problems for parents, including cyberbulling. Your computer can act as a dangerous conduit of malicious content directly to your child. One of the newest and most pervasive threats to a kid of the digital age is cyberbulling.

Cyberbullying is defined as actions that use information and communication technologies to support deliberate repeated, and hostile behavior by an individual or group that is intended to harm another or others. This can include harassing messages, spreading rumors online, or hacking into someone's account. It's important to make it clear to your child that they should feel no shame if this is happening to them and that they should let you know so you can both address the issue

Most parents of teenagers are concerned about what their teenage children do online and how their behavior could be monitored by others. Some parents are taking steps to observe, discuss, and check up on their children's' digital footprints..

Picture a young child with a bankruptcy on his record. Or a 17-year old who owns several houses and cars, and carries $750,000 worth of debt. The latter child's problems are the result of eight people fraudulently using her social security number. Imagine a driver's license in a baby's name. It's already happened, many times. And if you think grown-ups are the biggest target of identity thieves, think again. These stories are true cases of child identity theft related during a Federal Trade Commission discussion, "Stolen Futures: A forum on Child Identity Theft."

The number of reported child identity theft cases in the U.S. has increased by 200 percent since 2003, according to the Federal Trade Commission. A 2012 study found that one in 10 children has had his or her identity compromised.

Despite the increasing prevalence of this problem, more than 80 percent of parents with minor children say they are largely unfamiliar with child identity theft, according to a third-party research study.

It is important to be careful about how and why you share your child's information. Identity theft is a very personal crime, and it can take years to get a child's identity back after it's been stolen.

In the cyber-centric world of the 21st Century, parents have many risks and threats to ponder as they attempt to provide a safe present and a secure future for their children. Each day, a new danger seems to capture the headlines, from exposure to online predators to the cyber-bullying by schoolmates. Meanwhile, those parents are looking over their own shoulders, careful to guard against the crime of identity theft, so that they can continue to provide that safe present, and to build that secure future. Well, it just got worse.

It is possible that you could be quite effective at warding off online predators and cyber-bullies, as well as proving quite successful at guarding your own hard-earned good credit, only to find that your child's identity has been violated, and your family's financial and emotional well-being threatened in an almost inconceivable way.

What would you do if your child was in foreclosure on a home in another state? Wouldn't you want to know if your child had run up a huge utility bill across town?

These are not theoretical questions; these are real-life questions that the parents and guardians of children have been forced to come to grips with. In Child Identity Theft, you will find a hard look at what child identity theft means. I also list recommendations for preventative measures that should be taken by both public and private sector institutions, as well as protective steps for parents to take directly.

Discussing cyberbulling with your child is a great opportunity to discuss general cyber security protocol. Your identity and personal information are inherently threatened when you participate in the digital world. Part of teaching your kid to be smart about things like cyberbulling is teaching them to be smart about the dangers of the digital world.

Now you know some of the general cyber security problems and what cyberbulling is. What should your kid know? Below is a list of things your child should know about how to handle cyberbulling. Take the time to review these with your child and make sure they understand the importance of addressing cyberbulling in the correct manner.

- **Don't Respond:** The bully is trying to elicit a response: by responding you're empowering them.
- **Don't Retaliate:** Refusing to retaliate stops giving power to the bully and avoids the cycle of aggression..

- **Save the Evidence:** Hopefully by not engaging the bully the harassment stops, but it's important to save the evidence in case things escalate.

- **Talk to a Trusted Adult:** Whether it's you or another trusted adult, your kid deserves backup in this matter.

- **Block the Bully:** Many digital services give you the option to block the cyberbully. Do not hesitate to use this option.

- **Be Civil:** Don't sink to the bully's level. Plus, research shows that by gossiping and trash talking increases the likelihood of being bullied.

- **Don't be a Bully:** The golden rule still applies to the digital world. Just as in real life, treat others online how you wish to be treated.

- **Be a Friend, Not a Bystander:** If your child knows of cyberbulling happening to others, they should speak out against it and work out a solution to it.

- **Talk to an attorney to find out what other options may be available to you and your family.** Laws dealing with online harassment vary; it is important to discuss the matter with an attorney who knows the laws in your state or province.

Cyberbulling is an unfortunate use of new technology to harass youngsters, Parents need to talk to their kids about this topic and equip them with the skills and know-how to deal with it and ultimately stop it. By reviewing the tips above with your child and keeping the lines of communication open with them, you give your kids a better chance at avoiding the perils of cyberbulling.

The End of Childhood

From cyberbullying to sexting to prowling predators, the Information Age has brought with it a new spectrum of risks and threats for parents to guard their children against, and now that spectrum of threats has expanded to include child identity theft.

The online experience has changed childhood, for both better and worse. It enables children to explore the life of the world, but without proper precautions, it also enables the world to explore your child's life.

Consider a random sampling of news stories:

"Online bullying is a problem that affects almost half of all American teens, according to the National Crime Prevention Council. In a recent survey conducted by the Cyberbullying Research Center, 20 percent of middle-school students admitted to "seriously thinking about attempting suicide" as a result of online bullying." *MSNBC*

"More young children know how to play a computer game (58%) than ride a bike unaided (52%). While a quarter of young children can open a web browser window, just 20% can swim unaided. Incredibly, while over two-thirds (69%) of 2-5 year olds can operate a computer mouse, just 17% can tie their own shoelaces." *Biz Report*

"More than a quarter of young people have been involved in sexting in some form, an Associated Press-MTV poll found. ... Half of all young people said they have been targets of digital bullying." *Associated Press*

"Four out of five children can't tell when they are talking to an adult posing as a child on the internet, according to researchers working on software to track pedophiles online." *Science Daily*

With increased cyber awareness, individuals are seeking ways to secure their personal financial information more than ever before.

It's clear they need to go further and extend that protection for their children. Parents are already struggling to handle the threats of cyberspace, including securing their own computers and talking with their children about the many risks in cyberspace from online predators to cyberbullying. The trend in child identity theft is added weight on their shoulders. Although it will be a challenge for them to manage, it is essential to safeguarding their children's futures.

And now, to this troubling litany, add the issue of child identity theft

Implications and Consequences

Although the data's statistical significance is yet to be determined, it is certainly profoundly significant on a practical, human level to the thousands of children and families who have thus been victimized.

It is only common sense to surmise that the problem goes beyond those breached accounts included in this report, and that there are many thousands more children and their families at risk.

But even if it were only one child, what if that child were yours? Wouldn't you want to know your child was in foreclosure on a home in another state? Wouldn't you want to know if your child had run up a huge utility bill across town? Wouldn't you want to know that your child had a hunting license? Wouldn't you want to know that your child had a driver's license and a car registered in his or her name?

This information raises some serious questions. Wouldn't you want to know how this happened? And who was responsible? Was it the result of a security breach at a bank or a medical center or an online social media site? Was the perpetrator a petty cyber-criminal or an organized cyber-crime syndicate operating beyond our borders? Or was the perpetrator perhaps an insider, a family member or a close friend or a childcare worker? What recourse would you have?

Where would you turn? What would the long-term consequences be for you and your child? What would it take to undo the damage done? How would you know such a crime had occurred?

With the predictability of Social Security numbers there are two trends that, combined, are particularly worrisome: criminals are increasingly targeting minors' (even infants') SSNs for identity theft, and the SSNs of younger US residents are much easier to predict than the SSNs of those born before the 1990s. Our

Current identity-verification infrastructure is flawed and vulnerable, as it relies on authentication of numbers too widely available and too easy to compromise.

The Social Security Administration has begun assigning randomized number series as of June 25, 2011. Unfortunately, the more predictable Social Security numbers will remain in use.

Believe it or Not...

Here are some stranger than fiction facts that every parent should know.

- Many commercial and public sector entities do not treat Social Security numbers as unique identifiers. It is
- possible or one SSN to appear on more than one credit file, employment report, and criminal history – all mapped to different names.
- One reason that minor SSNs are so valuable is that there is currently no process for organizations, like employers or creditors to check what name and birth date is officially attached to this SSN. As long as an identity thief has a SSN

with a clear history, the thief can attach any name and birth date to it.

- In some cases parents can open utility bills under their Childs name and SSN to take advantage of their Childs clean SSN. Most parents do not intend to harm their Childs future, but in fact this is identity theft.

- When parents opt their children out of pre-approved credit card offers, it actually creates a credit file for the minor. These files cannot be deleted once created, but can be suppressed upon request of the parent. Parents need to contact each credit bureau regarding suppressing their Childs file.

- While parents try to deal with creditors to clean up issues, the creditors can ask to speak with the child -children as young as 1-2 years old – to verify their identity. Obviously creditors don't get very far using this method.

- Children with the same name as a parent are frequently mixed up with their parents credit file, causing them to have to deal with their same-name parents' credit - and any related issues. Mix-ups involving names can occur for different reasons including:
Certain information is reported and does not contain a SSN (for example, civil judgments). Collection agencies have been known to report debts only under name and address.

While it is not a requirement for children to obtain a SSN, most hospitals include applying for a SSN as one of the steps for parents to complete before leaving the hospital with their newborn.

Chapter **22**

Kids Privacy

The Children's Online Privacy Protection Act (COPPA), effective April 21, 2000, helps you protect your children's privacy. Enforced by the Federal Trade Commission, COPPA requires websites to get parental consent before collecting or sharing information from children who are under 13 years old. The new rules spell out what a Web site operator must include in a privacy policy and what responsibilities an operator has to protect children's privacy and safety online.

Take advantage of your COPPA rights. Your child's personal information is valuable, and you can do a lot to protect it.

Check Out Sites Your Kids Visit

If a site requires users to register, see what kind of information it asks for and determine your comfort level. You also can see whether the site appears to be following the most basic rules, like posting its privacy policy for parents clearly and conspicuously.

Review the privacy policy.

Just because a site has privacy policy doesn't mean it keeps personal information private. The policy can help you figure out if you're comfortable with what information the site collects and how it plans to use or share it. If the policy says there are no limits to what it collects or who gets to see it, there are no limits.

Ask questions.

If you have questions about a site's practices or policies, ask. The privacy policy should include contact information for someone prepared to answer your questions.

Know Your COPPA Rights

COPPA covers sites designed for kids under 13 and general audience sites that know certain users are under 13. COPPA protects information that websites collect upfront and information that your kids give out or post later.

COPPA requires privacy policies.

COPPA also requires these sites to post a privacy policy in a spot that's plain to see. The policy must provide details about what kind of information the site collects and what it might do with the information — for example, if it plans to use the information to target advertising to your kids or to give the information to other companies. The policy also should state whether those other companies have agreed to keep the information safe and confidential.

COPPA gives you the right to review collected information.

As the parent, you have a right to see any personal information a site has collected about your child. If you ask to see the information, website operators will need to make sure you really are the parent; they may choose to delete the information. You also have the right to retract your consent, and have any information collected about your child deleted.

You Can Be Picky with Your Permission

Websites can request your consent in a number of ways, including by email and postal mail. Before you give consent, make sure you know what information the site wants to collect and what it plans to do with it. And consider how much consent you want to give;

it's not an all or nothing proposition. You might give the company permission to collect some personal information, for example, but not allow them to share that information with others.

Report Any Site that Breaks the Rules
If you think a site has collected information from your kids or marketed to them in a way that violates the law, report it to the FTC at www.ftc.gov/complaint.

Talk to Your Kids

When your kids begin socializing online, you may want to talk to them about certain risks:

- Inappropriate conduct: The online world can feel anonymous. Kids sometimes forget that they are still accountable for their actions.
- Inappropriate contact: Some people online have bad intentions, including bullies, predators, hackers, and scammers.
- Inappropriate content: You may be concerned that your kids could find pornography, violence, or hate speech online.

You can reduce these risks by talking to your kids about how they communicate – online and off – and encouraging them to engage in conduct they can be proud of.

Talk Early and Often

The best way to protect your kids online? Talk to them. Research suggests that when children want important information, most rely on their parents.

Start early.

After all, even toddlers see their parents use all kinds of devices. As soon as your child is using a computer, a cell phone, or any mobile device, it's time to talk to them about online behavior, safety, and security. As a parent, you have the opportunity to talk to your kid about what's important before anyone else does.

Initiate conversations.

Even if your kids are comfortable approaching you, don't wait for them to start the conversation. Use everyday opportunities to talk to your kids about being online. For instance, a TV program featuring a teen online or using a cell phone can tee up a discussion about what to do — or not — in similar circumstances. And news stories about internet scams or cyberbullying can help you start a conversation about your kids' experiences and your expectations.

Create an Honest, Open Environment

Kids look to their parents to help guide them. Be supportive and positive. Listening and taking their feelings into account helps keep conversation afloat. You may not have all the answers, and being honest about that can go a long way.

Communicate Your Values

Be upfront about your values and how they apply in an online context. Communicating your values clearly can help your kids make smarter and more thoughtful decisions when they face tricky situations.

Be Patient

Resist the urge to rush through conversations with your kids. Most kids need to hear information repeated, in small doses, for it to sink in. If you keep talking with your kids, your patience and persistence will pay off in the long run. Work hard to keep the lines of communication open, even if you learn your kid has done something online you find inappropriate.

More Protection!

The Federal Trade Commission announced a landmark update to child privacy laws.
12/19/2012

Under the changes to the law, known as COPPA, websites, social media, online games and mobile apps will have to get parental permission to collect photos, videos and a wide array of other information that children expose online under new federal guidelines just released.

As evidence of online risks, the FTC said it was investigating an unspecified number of software developers that may have illegally gathered information without the consent of parents.

Aiming to prevent companies from exploiting online information about children under 13, the FTC imposed sweeping changes in regulations designed to protect a young generation with easy access to the Internet.

The FTC's update to child online privacy laws comes after a two-year debate over how far the government should go to protect the privacy of children 12 and younger without curbing the practices of a thriving Web economy that relies on data for advertising.

Information about children that cannot be collected unless a parent first gives permission now includes the location data that a cellphone generates, as well as photos, videos and audio files containing a human image or voice.

The amended rules to the decade-old Children's Online Privacy Protection Act went into effect on July 1.2103. Privacy advocates said the changes were long overdue in an era of cellphones, tablets, social networking services and online stores with cellphone apps aimed at kids for as little as 99 cents.

Siphoning details of children's personal lives — their physical location, contact information, names of friends and more — from their Internet activities can be highly valuable to advertisers, marketers and data brokers.

The rules offer several new methods of verifying a parent's consent, including electronically scanned consent forms, video conferencing and email.

Media and Silicon Valley giants such as Facebook and Disney have fought plans that they say would be difficult to implement and would stifle innovation. The FTC's chairman and public interest groups have said_an explosion of tracking tools and the swift adoption of smartphones and tablets in homes and schools have rendered the 1998 Children's Online Privacy Protection Act too weak.

The revisions, the FTC said, seek to clarify that much of today's most popular uses of the Web should be more closely guarded when done by children.

"The commission takes seriously its mandate to protect children's online privacy in this ever-changing technological landscape," FTC Chairman Jon Leibowitz said. "We think these rules are balanced and very, very strong."

Companies such as Google and Viacom must also have a parent's consent before using tracking tools, such as cookies, that use IP addresses and mobile device IDs to follow a child's Web activity across multiple apps and sites. Amassing that data could help a marketing company stitch together detailed profiles of children to be used to deliver tailored advertisements, a practice that should be spared on children, some privacy groups say.

Companies are not excluded from advertising on websites directed at children, allowing business models that rely on advertising to continue. But behavioral marketing techniques that target children are prohibited unless a parent agrees. Companies may not track children to build massive profiles.

The agency included in the rules new methods for securing verifiable consent after the software industry and Internet companies raised concerns over how to confirm that the permission actually came from a parent. Electronic scans of signed consent forms are acceptable, as is video-teleconferencing between the website operator or online service and the parent, according to the agency.

Emailed consent is also acceptable as long as the business confirms it by sending an email back to the parent or calling or sending a letter. In cases of email confirmation, the information collected can only be used for internal use by that company and not shared with third parties, the agency said.

The FTC's investigation of apps developers came after the agency examined 400 kids' apps that it purchased from Apple's iTunes store and Google's apps store, Google Play. It determined that 60 percent of them transmitted the user's unique device identification to the software maker or, more frequently, to advertising networks and companies that compile, analyze and sell consumer information for marketing campaigns.

In the end, the FTC decided that those companies would be liable only when they have "actual knowledge" that their partner sites are collecting information about children.

App stores such as Apple's iTunes and Google Play won't be liable for the child privacy practices of its hundreds of thousands of apps, the FTC said.

Leibowitz said violators of the rules will be subject to fines as high as $16,000 per incident.

Federal officials say the mobile apps space in particular has been a Wild West, where hundreds of apps aimed at children collected personal information and shared it with ad networks without informing parents

I applaud the FTC for its rigorous and comprehensive review of the (Children's Online Privacy Protection Act) rules and for bringing them up to date with industry changes, however, the commission will need to engage in ongoing monitoring efforts, as well as strong enforcement actions, if the implementation of these rules is to be effective in the long run. Parents, not social networks or marketers, will remain the gatekeepers when it comes to their children's privacy not only online but also on phones.

Chapter 23

Protecting Your Child's Identity

Keep Your Child's Personal Information Safe. Parents do a lot to protect their children from physical harm, from teaching them to look both ways before crossing the street to making sure they're dressed warmly for a snowy day. Protecting their personal information is important, too. Here's some easy steps to take to lessen the chance of your child falling victim to fraud:

- Don't make your child susceptible to "friendly" identity theft: Don't ever use your child's name to open utility or other credit accounts. Protect your child's personal information by keeping it locked up in your home where visitors cannot access it.

  • Keep all documents that show a child's personal information safely locked up. What is personal information? At a minimum, it includes a child's date of birth, Social Security number, and birth certificate. Gauge your child's level of responsibility before you share banking and credit information with them, even accounts in their name. Most children will need their Social Security card when they go off to college, but make sure they know to keep their card in a safe place rather than carry it around in a wallet or purse.

- Share your child's Social Security number only when you know and trust the other party. If someone asks for your child's Social Security number, ask why they want it, how they'll safeguard it, how long they'll keep it, and how they'll dispose of it. If you're not satisfied with the answers, don't share the number. Ask to use another identifier.

- Watch for mail in your child's name: If you begin receiving pre-approved credit cards or other unsolicited financial offers in your child's name, it is an indicator that your child may have an open credit file.

- Teach your child about identity theft and online safety: Talk to your child about the dangers of sharing personal data online. Children surfing the web are particularly vulnerable to exposing personal information in chat rooms or on social networking sites. Make sure children understand the importance of keeping this data private.

- Before you share personal information on the internet, make sure you have a secure connection. A secure website has a lock icon in the address bar and a URL that begins with "https."

- Use a computer with updated antivirus and firewall protection. Don't send personal or financial information – your child's or your own, for that matter – through an unsecured wireless connection in a public place.

- If you use a password to sign into a website, log out of the site when you're done on that site when you're done on that site.

- Limit the chances that your child's information will be stolen or misused at school. Find out who has access to your child's personal information, and read the notices that schools are required to send explaining your rights under the Family Durational Rights and Privacy Act (FERPA). That law protects the privacy of student education records, and gives you the right to opt out of the release of directory information to third parties, including other families.

Safely Dispose of Personal Information

Your trash could be a treasure trove of information for an identity thief. Before you get rid of information on paper or online, make sure no one else can use it.

Shred letters, forms, and other papers that include your child's personal information before you throw them out. For best results use a mechanical cross cut or Department of Defense (DOD) approved shredding device.

Delete electronic computer files that you no longer need, and empty your online trash or recycle bin.

Learn how to remove your personal or financial information that might be stored on your computer, cell phone, or other device before you dispose of it.

Share Safety Tips with Your Child

Your computer can hold enormous amounts of information, and it's crucial that it stays secure. Talk to your child about best practices for computer security, including:

• using "strong" passwords – those with at least fourteen characters, as well as numbers and symbols

• keeping passwords private

• knowing the risks of sharing files through peer to peer software, which may include giving someone access to more information on your computer than you want to share

• using anti-virus software that updates automatically

• being alert to phishing scams, where criminals send an email, text, or pop-up message that looks like it's from a legitimate organization. A phishing message asks the recipient to click on a link or call a phone number, and to share personal information for a prize or some other benefit. The message to kids: delete these messages without opening or responding.

Talk with your child regularly about the privacy settings on social media sites and what information and photos to share on them. For example, it's not a great idea to show photos with school or team uniforms, list birth dates or specific locations, or show background settings that are easy to identify. One reason? Someone can use the information posted on a social media profile to guess account passwords.

Protecting Your Child's Personal Information at School

Back to school — an annual ritual that includes buying new notebooks, packing lunches, coordinating transportation, and filling out forms: registration forms, health forms, permission slips, and emergency contact forms, to name a few. Many school forms require personal and, sometimes, sensitive information. In the wrong hands, this information can be used to commit fraud in your child's name. For example, a child's Social Security number can be used by identity thieves and other criminals to apply for government benefits, open bank and credit card accounts, apply for a loan or utility service, or rent a place to live.

The Federal Trade Commission (FTC), the nation's consumer protection agency, cautions that when children are victims of identity theft, the crime may go undetected for years — or at least until they apply for a job, a student loan or a car loan, or want to rent an apartment.

Limiting the Risks of Identity Theft

There are laws that help safeguard your child's and your family's personal information. For example, the federal Family Educational Rights and Privacy Act (FERPA), enforced by the U.S.

Department of Education, protects the privacy of student education records. It also gives parents of school-age kids the right to opt-out of sharing contact or other directory information with third parties, including other families.

If you're a parent with a child who's enrolled in school, the FTC suggests that you:

- **Find out who has access to your child's personal information,** and verify that the records are kept in a secure location.

- **Pay attention to materials sent home** with your child, through the mail or by email, that ask for personal information. Look for terms like "personally identifiable information," "directory information," and "opt-out." Before you reveal any personal information about your child, find out how it will be used, whether it will be shared, and with whom.

- **Read the annual notice schools must distribute that explains your rights under FERPA.** This federal law protects the privacy of student education records, and gives you the right to:
    - Inspect and review your child's education records;
    - Consent to the disclosure of personal information in the records; and
    - Ask to correct errors in the records.

- **Ask your child's school about its directory information policy.** Student directory information can include your child's name, address, date of birth, telephone number, email address, and photo. FERPA requires schools to notify parents and guardians about their school directory policy, and give you the right to opt-out of the release of directory information to third parties. It's best to put your request in writing and keep a copy for your files. If you don't opt-out, directory information may be available not only to the people in your child's class and school, but also to the general public.

- **Ask for a copy of your school's policy on surveys.** The Protection of Pupil Rights Amendment (PPRA) gives you the right to see surveys and instructional materials before they are distributed to students.

- **Consider programs that take place at the school but aren't sponsored by the school.** Your child may participate in programs, like sports and music activities, that aren't formally sponsored by the school. These programs may have web sites where children are named and pictured. Read the privacy policies of these organizations, and make sure you understand how your child's information will be used and shared.

- **Take action if your child's school experiences a data breach.** Contact the school to learn more. Talk with teachers, staff, or administrators about the incident and their practices. Keep a written record of your conversations. Write a letter to the appropriate administrator, and to the school board, if necessary.

File a complaint

You may file a written complaint with the U.S. Department of Education. Contact the Family Policy Compliance Office, U.S. Department of Education, 400 Maryland Ave., SW, Washington, DC 20202-5920, and keep a copy for your records.

Chapter 24

Warning Signs of Child Identity Theft

Personal circumstances may increase the risk of child identity theft – an adult in financial hot water, for example, may think "adopting" a child's identity is a way to start over. But using someone else's identity, regardless of the reason, is a crime. Identity theft can be committed by a family member, a neighbor, or by someone you never met who gets access to your child's information. Several signs can tip you off to a problem:

• You get calls from collection agencies, bills from credit card companies or medical providers, or offers for credit cards or bank account checks in your child's name, even if your child has never applied for or used
these services.

• Your child, or your family, is denied government benefits because benefits are being paid to another account that is using your child's Social Security number.

• The Social Security Administration, Internal Revenue Service (IRS), or some other government agency asks you to confirm that your child is employed, even though your child has never had a job.

• After you file a tax return listing your dependent child's name and Social Security number, you get notice from the IRS that the same information is listed on another tax return.

• Your child gets a notice from the IRS saying he or she failed to pay taxes on income, even though your child has no income.

Does Your Child Have a Credit Report?

You may want to check whether your child has a credit report. Decide how often to check based on whether you think information is at risk. For example, if you see warning signs, lost your child's Social Security card, had a break-in, or your child's information was compromised in a data breach, you may want to check whether there is a report using your child's name or information. Check at least as often as the law entitles you to do it for free.

It's a good idea to check whether your child has a credit report close to the child's 16th birthday, which is probably before the child applies for a tuition or car loan, apartment, or job. If you find a report with errors, you can work on correcting the errors before the child needs credit.

There are three nationwide credit reporting companies:

Equifax
1-800-525-6285

Experian
1-888-397-3742

TransUnion
1-800 680-7289

Contact each credit reporting company and ask it to search to see if your child has a credit report. Each company will check for files related to your child's name and Social Security number, and also for files related only to the Social Security number. You must provide the credit reporting companies with proof that you are the child's parent or legal guardian.

Ask each company to search for your child's credit report.

Ask for a manual search based only on the child's Social Security number.

Provide proof that you are the child's parent or legal guardian.

Include a cover letter with the child's full name, date of birth, and home addresses for the last five years.

The credit reporting companies may require copies of:
the child's birth certificate listing the parents
the child's Social Security card
your government-issued identification card, like a driver's license
or military identification, or copies of documents proving you are the child's legal guardian
proof of your address, like a utility bill, or a credit card or insurance statement

Chapter 25

Your Child's Identity Has Been Stolen: What Now?

Sometimes, no matter how diligent you are about protecting personal information, it gets lost, stolen, or hacked.

If that happens, follow these steps:

1. Alert Each Credit Reporting Company

Contact each of the three nationwide credit reporting companies.

Explain that your child is a minor, and can't legally enter into any type of contract. Ask each company for its mailing address. To prove that your child is a minor, send the credit reporting companies a completed copy of the Uniform Minor's Status Declaration *(see page 143)* or found online at: http://www.ftc.gov/bcp/edu/pubs/consumer/idtheft/idto 8.pdf

Next, send a letter to each credit reporting company. Ask them to remove all accounts, account inquiries, and collection notices from the credit file associated with your child's name or personal information.

HOW TO ALERT THE CREDIT REPORTING COMPANIES

Contact each credit reporting company.

Explain to each company that your child is a minor.

Provide proof that your child is a minor.

Send each of the credit reporting companies a completed copy of the Uniform Minor's Status Declaration *(see page 139)* or found online: www.ftc.gov/bcp/edu/pubs/consumer/idtheft/idt08.pdf

Send a letter to each credit reporting company.

Ask them to remove all items associated with your child's name or personal information, including:
accounts - account inquiries - collection notices

2. Place an Initial Fraud Alert

If a credit file was created for your child as a result of identity theft, consider placing an initial fraud alert on the credit file. An initial fraud alert requires potential creditors to verify a person's identity before extending credit. When a creditor knows that a minor is involved, it will not ordinarily extend credit.

To place an initial fraud alert, contact any one of the three credit reporting companies. The company you contact must contact the other two companies. All three will place an initial fraud alert on the file they have for your child. After you place the initial fraud alert, the credit reporting company will explain your rights, including your right to get a free copy of your child's credit report from each credit reporting company.

HOW TO PLACE A FRAUD ALERT

Contact one credit reporting company.

Ask the company to put a fraud alert on your child's credit file.

Confirm that the company you call will contact the other two companies.

Report that your minor child is an identity theft victim.
Ask each company to put a freeze on the child's credit file

Provide proof that you are the child's parent or legal guardian.
The credit reporting companies may request copies of: the child's birth certificate - the child's Social Security number, documents proving you are the child's parent or legal guardian.

Ask each company for its mailing address.

Pay a fee.
Pay any fee required by state law.

Mark your calendar.
Your state law determines how long the credit freeze lasts.

3. File a Report with the FTC

File an identity theft report at www.ftc.gov or call 1-877-438-4338. Provide as many details about the theft as possible. Save a copy of the completed complaint, this is called an Identity Theft Affidavit. If you file a police report, give a copy of the Affidavit to the police.

HOW TO REPORT IDENTITY THEFT TO THE FTC

ONLINE OPTION

Complete the FTC's online complaint form.
www.ftc.gov/complaint

Fill out the complaint form. Include as many details as possible.
When the form is complete, click "Submit."
After you submit your information, you will see a complaint reference number. Save this number.

Save or print the completed complaint.
After you submit your information, print a copy of the completed complaint or save it electronically. The completed complaint is your Identity Theft Affidavit.

Update the complaint.
If you need to add details to your complaint, call the FTC and give the complaint reference number.

BY PHONE OPTION

Call the FTC. 1-877-438-4338

Tell the representative what happened.

The representative will give you a complaint reference number, and an Affidavit password, and send you an email explaining how to get your Affidavit.

Follow the directions in the email. Print a copy of your completed complaint and save it electronically. The completed complaint is your Identity Theft Affidavit.

Update the complaint.

If you need to add details to your complaint, call the FTC and give the complaint reference number.

Consider Filing a Police Report

Usually, adults must file a police report about identity theft before they can use certain legal remedies to clear a credit report. The situation may be different for children, because credit reporting companies may correct a child victim's credit file without a police report. Send credit reporting companies a Uniform Minor's Status Declaration *(see page 139)* _ or a letter explaining that your child is a minor who cannot legally enter into a contract. After you provide proof that the victim is a minor, credit reporting companies and businesses should correct the fraudulent information that the identity thief created.

It's important to file a police report if you need to resolve a child victim's medical, tax-related, or other identity theft.

HOW TO FILE A POLICE REPORT

Go to your local police department or the police department where the theft occurred.

Bring a copy of your Identity Theft Affidavit and any other proof of the theft.

Complete a report about the theft.

Get a copy of the report, or the report number.

Call Every Company Where an Account Was Fraudulently Opened or Misused

If you already know where your child's information was misused, contact the company. Ask it to close the fraudulent account and flag the account to show it is a result of identity theft.

Otherwise, when you receive your child's credit report, review it for any accounts opened with the child's name or personal information. If you see a fraudulent account in your child's name, contact the company where the account was opened. Ask the company to close the fraudulent account and flag the account to show it is the result of identity theft.

If your child has a college savings, bank, or credit union account, monitor the account statements. If you see an account was misused, ask the financial institution's fraud department to restore any erroneous withdrawals and flag the account to show it was compromised by identity theft. For more help, contact the Agency that oversees the financial institution about your child's rights.
Get information at w.ffiec.gov/consumercenter/default.aspx.

After you contact a business, follow up in writing, and enclose a completed copy of the Uniform Minor's Status Declaration. *(See page 139)*

UNIFORM MINOR'S STATUS DECLARATION

This is a voluntary declaration for establishing that a child is a minor. Use it for disputes with credit reporting companies and creditors about identity theft-related problems.

ABOUT THE MINOR CHILD

Full Legal Name

_____

| Last, Suffix | First | Middle |

Date of Birth _____ **SSN** _____
　　　　　　　　　　mm/dd/yy

Current Street Address

_____

_____

| City | State | Zip |

The child has lived at this address since

_____
　　　　　mm/dd/yy

All other addresses where the child has lived within the last five years:

_____

_____

_____

_____

Should a Child Identity Theft Victim Get a New Social Security Number?

The Social Security Administration may assign a new Social Security number to your child if:

• the child is being harassed, abused, or is in grave danger when using the original number

• you can prove that someone has stolen the number and is using it illegally. You must provide evidence that the number actually is being misused, and that the misuse is causing the child significant, continuing harm.

If you apply for a new Social Security number for your child, you must prove the child's age, citizenship or lawful immigration status, and identity.

Getting a new Social Security number probably won't resolve all problems related to the theft of your child's identity. Government agencies and some businesses may keep records under the child's original Social Security number. In addition, because credit reporting companies use Social Security numbers and other personal information to identify a person's credit file, using a new number doesn't guarantee a fresh start. But, by being careful with your child's personal information and monitoring credit reports for fraudulent activity, you can limit the misuse. Learn more at www.socialsecurity.gov or call 1-800-722-1213.

Medical Identity Theft

A thief may use a child's identity to get medical services. Read the explanation of benefits statements your insurance company sends you each time it pays for service in your child's name. If you get a statement for services your child did not receive, contact the medical provider. Get a copy of the medical records, and ask the medical provider to remove or segregate all charges and services that are not related to your child. Be sure that the medical provider flags any of your child's accounts that were compromised by identity theft. Follow up in writing and enclose a completed copy of the Uniform Minor's Status Declaration *(See page 143)*

Tax-Related Identity Theft

If your child gets a notice from the IRS for unpaid taxes, even though he or she never earned income, or you get a notice from the IRS saying your child's name and Social Security number were listed on another return, your child may be a victim of tax-related identity theft. If you or your child gets such a notice, respond immediately to the address included with the IRS notice. The IRS never makes a first contact with taxpayers by email, and doesn't ask for detailed personal information through email. If you get an email that claims to be from the IRS, call the IRS (1-800-829-1040) and ask if they sent the message.

If you learn that an identity thief used your child's Social Security number on a tax return, call the IRS Specialized Identity Theft Protection Unit (1-800-908-4490).

If you think your child's information may be at risk, you can ask the IRS to monitor the use of your child's Social Security number for suspicious activity. You will have to complete an IRS Identity Theft Affidavit (IRS Form 14039) and send a copy of an identity document, like a Social Security card, passport, or driver's license.

-Federal Trade Commission -

New Alert:

Predators Using Online Photos to Target Children

Uploading pictures of your children playing at the park or in your backyard to social media or photo sharing websites could put them at risk. Most smart phones and many newer digital cameras use GPS to tag your pictures with the exact location where they were taken. When shared publicly, this information can be used by predators to locate your child within a few feet. An album full of tagged pictures can provide a map of locations where your child might be vulnerable.

The best way to avoid this danger is to disable GPS tagging on your smart phone or camera. Check your settings or contact your cell phone provider for assistance if you are unsure how to do so.

Chapter 26

Bottom Line

If it were only one child, it would be one too many. But the FTC documents over three and a half million children, and there are likely many more. Unfortunately Child Identity Theft is impossible to prevent. Children should not have a credit report, and fraud alerts cannot be placed on a report that does not exist.

Taking proactive measures to prevent childhood identity theft provides a sense of relief and security that cannot be underestimated. By protecting your child's identity, you are removing the potential for an enormous amount of suffering and hardship when they reach adulthood and encounter the problem on their own. Enrolling in college, beginning a career, starting a family – all become immensely difficult when your child is digging out from under the burden of restoring his or her credit history and reclaiming his or her identity.

This is disturbing evidence concerning the nature and appeal of child identity theft, and highlights some real risks and threats, e.g.:

- *10.2% is a significant rate and is dramatically higher than the attack rate for adults. Parents need to think about their children's future, and take the time to look into this frequently overlooked problem*

- *Take steps to protect your children, especially in advance of key financial milestones like student* loans, college, first job, apartment rental
- *Even though some identity theft results from non-malicious things like mixed credit files, the results are the same for parents and children. All child identity theft can result in credit, financial, and identity issues that greatly impact a child's* future including school loans, job opportunities, *and more*

Meanwhile, institutions in both the public and private sector need to address the issue of child identity theft more aggressively.

And whether or not any action is taken on either of these fronts, parents must be proactive.

They say knowledge is power, and the more we know the better we can do. Today, it's important to recognize that even though our children may not be using their SSN's to obtain credit or employment; *someone else might be...*

Put plainly, it is not simply enough to guard your own identity in the 21st Century; you must also guard your child's.

<u>Part Three</u>

It's Time for a Peace of Mind

Now you know the problem so let's start solving it.

One of the most interesting facts I learned from writing this book is that most people think "It will never happen to me." If you have read to this point, you sincerely want to protect your most valuable asset. As a thank-you for the time you have invested, this last section is designed to be a bonus for you – questions and answers, along with a heartfelt recommendation.

Frequently Asked Questions

Q: *What makes* ***"Deploy Predator Surveillance"*** *different from any other books on identity theft?*

A: Unlike most books on Identity Theft, ***"Deploy Predator Surveillance"*** is written to be easily understood by anyone. Most are written to show how smart the author is rather than make the information useful and relevant to the average person (as opposed to academics, attorneys or technologists). ***Deploy Predator Surveillance*** also puts the issues in perspective for businesses regarding what they need to do and why. In the end, it is about connecting the dots as to what the problems are, why they matter to you, as an individual or as a business owner, and what you can do about it.

Q: *My health insurance provider insists on using my Social Security number (SSN) as my subscriber ID number. Is there a law that prohibits this?*

A: Given the number of lost and stolen wallets, this practice places many of us at higher risk for identity theft. Some states have passed laws that prohibit the use of the Social Security number as a personal identifier. One thing you can do is photocopy your card, front and back, cut off the last 4 numbers of the Social Security Number from the copy and carry the copy with you on a daily basis. Employers can also request that their health providers use alternate subscriber numbers.

Q: *My employer posts our Social Security Number on our timecards. They can be seen by everyone who works there and are by the public restrooms. Could this put me in danger?*

A: Anytime an employer places your Social Security Number on a timecard, document, report, purchase receipt or ID badge it adds to your risk factor. Another poor practice is the use of the Social Security Number as a password/computer login. You should request a change in policy. This could be considered negligent behavior and opens companies up for a potential lawsuit. Again, some states are passing laws that prohibit the public display of Social Security Number.

Q: The enrollment form our new school district uses requests my Social Security Number. Why would they need that? Do I have to give it to them?

A: It is always a good idea to ask why information is needed before providing it. The answer – it's on the form – is not a valid answer. You need to find out the reason behind the request. If the child's health insurance number is your Social Security Number then they might need it for emergency purposes. Otherwise, it doesn't seem reasonable. I have found several school districts that asked for that information. After questioning the practice, the parents were told that it was an optional field.

Q: What is the best way to convince the company that I work for that some of the things they do are placing employees and customers in danger of identity theft?

A: Many companies are reluctant to change old practices due to the cost involved but also because it might be construed as admitting they were negligent in some way. I have found the best approach is to acknowledge that the world has changed, and therefore security measures must be updated accordingly.

Your company must be shown that the problem of identity theft has forced ALL of us to reconsider our information handling practices – consumer and corporations alike. Companies that take these steps are often able to show the public that they are a responsible, caring business with the best interests of employees and the public at heart.

Q: I am a new victim of identity theft. I think the imposter works for the same company that I do. What do I do?

A: Since sensitive information including the Social Security Number and even bank account numbers are so accessible in the workplace, security breaches at work are a common way for identity thieves to gather information. I advise companies to write a policy regarding workplace identity theft reporting and post it in a conspicuous spot. The policy should provide a way for any victim of identity theft, company-related or not, to confidentially report the crime. Since HR is where the most information is stored, and therefore an attractive spot for an identity thief, reports should be redirected to the Security, Operations or the Chief Privacy Officer. Since most victims don't know how the thief got the information, this gives the company a chance to evaluate whether the crimes seem similar. If the crime is an internal theft, the company needs to notify the appropriate law enforcement authorities. Unless told otherwise by the authorities they should then notify affected employees and members of the public.

Q: Do you have a model policy letter that our company can use?

A: Yes. Feel free to modify it. You will find it in this section of my website: Workplace Model Letter
DeployPredatorSurveillance.com

Q: *Why should I get training for all my employees?*

A: As we discuss in the training, you would be amazed at the circumstances that would allow people who wouldn't normally have access to sensitive information to gain access to it. In the end, do you really want to explain why the person you didn't train is the one who lost the information (for further information, see Murphy's Law).

Q: *Who are your best Audiences?*

A: Let me answer that at two levels. Every person with a Social Security number is at risk of identity theft, which means that nearly everyone can benefit from my presentation. One in ten households will experience identity theft this year with an average cost of recovery of $7,500 and several hundred hours. The risk can be drastically reduced by implementing a combination of common sense and targeted tools.

But at another level (which entails business profitability and responsibility), organizations bring me in because they need their employees or members to understand the value of the private data that they handle every day. Whether it's a client's credit card number, a patient's medical file, employee records or sensitive intellectual capital, our economy is built on information. If employees and executives ignore the inherent value of that information (and the resulting liabilities of collecting, storing and handling it), then we can never expect them to protect it. I get them to understand the value of those assets.

When I inspire the audience to think twice about company privacy, your return on investment (by preventing a costly data breach) can be remarkable. Companies that proactively train their employees about data privacy significantly lower the chances of a costly data breach. I like to say that safe data is profitable data. Companies like Target, Home Depot, Staples, Chase Bank, Anthem-BlueCross/BlueShield   and www.AnnualCreditReport.com (*who had a data breach of 200 million identities*) learned the hard way about the profitability of privacy. My audiences understand that before it happens.

Q. *How does your audience feel when they walk out the door?*

A: Motivated to protect their privacy and empowered with the tools to make it happen. I show them what can happen to the person on the other end of that "data" if it disappears. I don't sell fear, but give a voice to reality. And I don't come at it from the perspective of law enforcement or techno-babble. The audience leaves with the motivation not only to protect themselves and their families, but the sensitive data they handle every day in the workplace. In fact, they understand that their jobs depend on it.

Q: I am applying for a new job. The application requests my driver's license and Social Security numbers. Due to the increasing amount of identity theft, I would rather not disclose that information until I am offered the job. Do you have a recommendation on how to handle this situation?

A: I asked several HR people for their answers:

- If a job applicant did not want to share their Social Security Number at the time of the interview, I would certainly understand, especially if they shared with me the reason why. If someone told me they had been a victim of identity theft, I would not press the issue nor would I reject their chance to be interviewed. I can't imagine any employer refusing an interview on that basis. If they do, then it may be a violation of "equal opportunity for employment" law. Due to tax laws, once chosen, the candidate would then have to submit his or her Social Security Number.
- Where it says Social Security Number, place "Available upon request" or "See below" and explain your reason at the bottom of the form. You may say that due to high incidence of identity theft crime, you prefer to provide it directly to the interviewer.

"I would like to believe that all employers are as forward thinking as the ones that responded. That is not true and this is a situation where consumers need to make a hard decision. The reality is, fair or not, your desire to protect your information could cost you employment."

Q: I am a victim of identity theft. I am still trying to remove the imposter's actions from my credit reports and think he may have gotten a ticket in my name. What do I tell a potential employer since I know they will do a background search prior to hiring me?

A: If the company has shown some interest in hiring you (they don't do background searches until then) then share that you are a victim of identity theft and that a background search may not be completely accurate. Explain that you are still working "on your own time" to remove his actions from your reports. Any police reports or official documents (statements from credit issuers) you have will help the interviewer understand the problem. Request that you have a chance to go over the results of the search to make sure it is accurate and reflects your true information. States are starting to pass laws that would require employers to share this information with you.

"These answers should not be used in lieu of legal advice. If you do not have an attorney as a Licensed Legal Services Agent, I would be glad to make a recommendation."

Conclusion

The greatest fear we face is our APATHY! Remember, don't bury you head in the sand with regards to identity theft. The fact that you read this book signifies that you won't. You have learned what it really is and why it matters to you. A lot of people fail to take any action and far too many end up regretting it... just ask the 10 million plus American victims each year.

In recent years, some identity theft monitoring services have been criticized for misleading marketing and exaggerated protection guarantees. One of the largest and most highly advertised companies has agreed to pay $11 million to the FTC and $1 million to a group of 35 state attorney generals to settle charges that the company's claims of providing 100-percent protection against identity theft were false. The company promised consumers complete protection against all types of identity theft, in truth, the protection it provided left enough holes that you could drive a truck thru it. **No Identity Theft plan will prevent identity theft,** but a few can serve as an early warning system so you can prevent further harm from occurring. Remember, the key to prevention is knowledge and using common sense. You must learn as much as you can about identity theft to truly protect yourself.

After months and months of extensive research, as a benefits coordinator, I recommend that you **INVEST IN IDENTITY THEFT PROTECTION;** An Identity Theft plan will provide you with peace of mind by leveraging experts, experience, and technology to monitor, protect, and restore your identity. <u>Find one that offers all of the following areas of coverage for Complete & Secure Protection:</u>

- **World Wide Coverage** – Offices in over 50 cities in 22 countries. The global leader in risk mitigation and response solutions.

- **$5 Million Service Guarantee** - They will do whatever it takes, for as long as it takes, to get a member's identity back should someone compromise it.
- **Member, Spouse, and Children Covered** – Monitoring up to eight unmarried children living at home until age twenty six,
- **Continuous Credit Bureau Monitoring** – Monitoring and reporting, online access to reports, alerts of credit activity such as new inquiries, new trade lines or derogatory events and new public record or address changes
- **Unlimited Identity Theft Consultation** – Members have unlimited access to speak with experts on any matter relating to identity theft

Plus, Total Comprehensive Restoration. By signing a *limited power of attorney* members are provided a dedicated **Licensed Fraud Investigator** who will help them to do such things as:
- Open a fraud case, including a credit report
- Gather and complete all necessary paperwork, including police reports
- Investigate emergent and potentially complicated trails of fraudulent activity
- Determine if creditors extended credit due to misuse of identifying information
- Notify and work with collection agencies holding fraudulent accounts
- Contact creditors and collection agencies to dispute all fraudulent accounts
- Issue fraud alert packets to all appropriate parties such as creditors, credit bureaus, Social Security Administration, etc.
- Interact with affected financial institutions and credit card companies and prepare appropriate documents

- Monitor identity status once restoration is complete and the case is closed, including examination of tri-merged credit report to ensure the member's identity has been restored to pre-theft status

Combined with a Legal Access Plan

Regardless of your choice, whether it is a do-it-yourself, a professional identity protection company, credit monitoring, legal services plan or some combination of these, the important thing is that you take action now to protect yourself and your loved ones

Even if you choose not to follow my advice, at least you will know where you may be putting yourself at risk.

Pay it Forward.

Rodney Holder

Resources

Federal Bureau of Investigation (FBI) – fbi.gov
The FBI, a criminal law enforcement agency, investigates cases of identity theft. The FBI recognizes that identity theft is a component of many crimes, including bank fraud, mail fraud, bankruptcy fraud, insurance fraud, fraud against the government, and terrorism. Local field offices are listed in the Blue pages of your phone directory

Federal Trade Commission (FTC)
The Federal Trade Commission is the agency tasked with stemming the tide of identity theft and helping businesses and consumers protect themselves and each other from the results of these crimes. Many of the best resources available on identity theft were created by them and are readily available to you. How should you as a consumer respond to becoming a victim, It's here. Basic guides to protecting your company, It's here.

FTC Identity Theft Homepage - www.ftc.gov/bcp/edu/microsites/idtheft
This is the home page for FTC information regarding Identity Theft. If you are not sure what you want to see, this is a great starting point.

Identity Theft Resource Center (ITRC) - www.idtheftcenter.org

The Identity Theft Resource Center is a national, non-profit organization designed to provide free suggestions to consumers and victims about what they can do about identity theft.

Internal Revenue Service (IRS) - www.irs.gov/uac/Identity-Protection

The IRS is committed to working with taxpayers who are the victims of identity theft. We are continually looking at ways to increase data security and protect taxpayers' identities with assistance from our Identity Protection Specialized Unit. Identity theft cases are among the most complex ones we handle.

National Consumers League -http://www.fraud.org/
This is the website of National Consumers League. They have
great information on how to fight con artist and scams. They even
provide consumers a complaint form to report suspicious fraud
activities. Great helpful information on telemarketing fraud,
elderly scams, online fraud and scams and updated news.

Office of Inspector General (OIG) –
www.oig.hhs.gov
The Health and Human Services is the largest inspector
general's office in the Federal Government. A majority of
the **OIG's** resources goes toward the oversight of Medicare
and Medicaid.

Privacy Rights Clearinghouse -
www.privacyrights.org
This site contains a chronology of data breaches and total
number of people that have been affected.

The President's Task Force on Identity Theft
www.idtheft.gov/

Established on May 10, 2006 to fight Identity theft. The website
has some very useful information on how to combat Identity theft
and how to report them. They also offer the Guide for Assisting
Identity Theft Victims (Guide) to help lawyers and victims of
identity theft victims on how to resolve identity theft legal issues.

USA.gov - www.usa.gov/Citizen/Topics/Internet-Fraud.shtml
This USA.gov website has valuable information on how to fight
Internet fraud. They have various list of government web
resources to help in reporting and or simply learning about
internet fraud. They have information on how to prevent internet
fraud, how to report them, phishing scams, internet protection for
consumers and businesses, cybercrime, spyware and more.

For More Information
Free Credit Reports

Consumers nationwide can get three free credit reports a year – one from each of the three credit bureaus: Equifax, Experian, and TransUnion – to watch for signs of identity theft and other types of fraud. I recommend staggering the requests so that one report is issued every four months. That way, you can monitor your credit reports on an ongoing basis.

Order by phone: (877) 322-8228

Order online: www.AnnualCreditReport.com

By mail: P.O. Box 105281, Atlanta, GA 30348-5281

Remember, if you have been the victim of credit fraud [15 USC 1681j (b) or are denied credit [15 USC 1681j (c)] you are entitled to a free credit report. If you are a victim of fraud, be sure to ask the credit bureaus for free copies. They will often provide them.

Credit Reporting Bureaus - Fraud Divisions

Equifax:

P.O. Box 740250, Atlanta, GA 30374

Report a Fraud: (800) 525-6285

Online Fraud alert: www.fraudalerts.equifax.com

Experian (formerly TRW):

P.O. Box 1017, Allen TX 75013

Report a Fraud: (888) 397-3742

Online Fraud alert: www.experian.com/fraud

TransUnion:

PO Box 6790, Fullerton, CA 92634

Report Fraud: (800) 680-7289

Online Fraud alert: www.transunion.com/personal-credit/credit-disputes/fraud-alerts.page

Direct Marketing

Opt out of pre-approved offers of credit or marketing lists by contacting:

OptOut Prescreen: www.optoutprescreen.com

Phone: (888) 567-8688

Remove your name from mail or phone lists by writing to:

Direct Marketing Association: www.dmachoice.org

Mail Preference Service:

P.O. Box 9008, Farmingdale, NY 11735

Personal Check Fraud Help

Check Rite: (701) 214- 4123

CrossCheck: (800) 552-1900

Chexsystems: (800) 428-9623

Telecheck: (800) 710-9898

On Guard On Line
This site is geared to help raise the awareness of young people on the issues of privacy, data protection and identity theft. It is geared toward activities online and includes games and other interactive tools that make it more interesting. www.onguardonline.gov/

Privacy and Data Protection
This page shows how the FTC seeks out and prosecutes companies that violate Federal law or fail to provide proper protections for customer privacy. www.ftc.gov/privacy/

Protecting Personal Privacy: A guide for Business
This guide for business is a great start for understanding what you have to do to protect your organization. While this guide was not the basis for our products and services, our services will help you meet almost all of these requirements. www.ftc.gov/infosecurity/

Red Flag Rules
This FTC description of the Red Flags Rule includes general guidance on how to meet the requirements of the Rule. While this resource is a good guide to understanding the Rule, making your program more than just a compliance requirement you have to meet requires more. www.ftc.gov/bcp/edu/pubs/business/idtheft/bus23.shtm

Special Publication 800-122 Guide to Protecting the Confidentiality of Personally Identifiable Information (PII)

While NIST is charged with providing standards and guidance to the Federal government, this guide can serve as a valuable tool for any organization seeking to prioritize the use of security dollars regarding protecting PII. csrc.nist.gov/publications/nistpubs/800-122/sp800-122.pdf

Taking Charge
This is the definitive guide for how to recover from Identity Theft. In particular, there are some interesting facts inside that may make it clear exactly how severe the problem of Identity Theft can be. www.ftc.gov/bcp/edu/pubs/consumer/idtheft/idt04.shtm

Law Overview

This resource is a list of and description of the Federal statutes that pertain directly to Identity Theft as well as other potentially useful articles and resources www.llrx.com/features/idtheftguide.htm

Fair and Accurate Credit Transaction Act (FACTA)
This revision to the Fair Credit Reporting Act includes the mandate to create the Red Flags Rule as well penalties for failure to properly dispose of sensitive data. These changes apply to almost every employer. www.privacyrights.org/fs/fs6a-facta.htm

Fair Credit Reporting Act (FCRA)
The omnibus law regarding privacy in the United States, FCRA is the basis for almost all businesses on how to manage privacy. www.ftc.gov/os/statutes/031224fcra.pdf

Health Insurance Portability and Administration Act (HIPAA)
The most important pieces of HIPAA are the Privacy and Security Rules. They provide guidance for care and usage of sensitive health data.
www.hhs.gov/ocr/privacy/hipaa/understanding/index.html
www.hhs.gov/ocr/privacy/hipaa/administrative/privacyrule/adminsimpregtext.pdf

HIPAA Privacy Rule
www.hhs.gov/ocr/privacy/hipaa/administrative/privacyrule/adminsimpregtext.pdf

HIPAA Security Rule
www.hhs.gov/ocr/privacy/hipaa/administrative/securityrule/securityrulepdf.pdf

HITECH Act
This law expanded the applicability of HIPAA to include Business Associates. It is also the first Federal Breach Notification Law, covering Sensitive Health Information.

www.hhs.gov/ocr/privacy/hipaa/understanding/coveredentiti
es/federalregisterbreachrfi.pdf

Red Flags Rule
Developed by the Federal Trade Commission and other
financial regulatory agencies, the Red Flags Rule is intended
to help organizations prevent fraud and protect themselves
and their customers. It applies to almost every organization,
but serves as sound guidance even for those organizations that
are not required to follow it.
www.ftc.gov/os/fedreg/2007/november/071109redflags.pdf

Department of Justice (DOJ) – www.usdoj.gov
The DOJ and its U.S Attorneys prosecute federal identity theft
cases. Information on identity theft is available at
www.usdoj.gov / criminal / fraud / idtheft.html

U.S. Secret Service (USSS) – www.tres,gov / usss
The U.S. Secret Service investigates financial crimes, which
may include identity theft. Although the Secret Service
generally investigates cases where the dollar loss is
substantial, your information may provide evidence of a larger
pattern of fraud requiring their involvement.

Local field offices are listed in the Blue pages of your telephone
directory.
Financial Crime Division -
www.tres.gov / usss / financial_crimes.shtml

Educate and Protect Others

"SHARE THIS BOOK"

Identity theft is a perennial crime that has taken on new dimensions in the Information Age. Taking proactive measures to prevent Identity Theft and Data Breaches provides a sense of relief that cannot be underestimated.

Many times we get asked if there are any price breaks for large quanity of books for groups. For this reason, Rodney is willing to *Pay It Forward* and offer special quanity discounts for your group or organization. $16.95

Special Quanity Discounts

12-24 Books	$11.00 each
25-99 Books	$10.00 each
100 – 499 Books	$9.00 each
500 - 999 Books	$8.00 each
1000+ Books	$7.00 each

Rodney Holder 205-310-7255

SPECIAL OFFER!

Protect your personal information against technologically savvy thieves by using the **RFID Secure Sleeve.** Almost 200 Million credit and debit cards have been embedded with radio frequency chips (RFID chips) that store personal Information. However, over the next 2-3 years, it is expected that credit card issuers will replace every single magnetic stripe credit and debit card with a new contactless smartcard, and why shouldn't they? The new cards seem to make it all easier. So much easier that some folks are reading your credit cards before you even take them out of your wallet. Unfortunately, this makes consumers more susceptible to identity theft. **It was recently featured on FoxNews, CNN, Inside Edition, Discovery Channel, and countless local news stations** educating the public on how easy it is to use. This lightweight RFID Blocking Sleeve is made using a patented process with special alloy that is the perfect solution for protecting yourself against scanning and electronic pickpocketing.

FIVE for only $10.00

PURCHASE HERE:
DeployPredatorSurveillance.com

"They have given me more than I could have ever given them."

Pearls for Parents

From a single guy with over 700 Kids!

50 Gems to comfort, encourage, inspire and warm your hearts!

Rodney Holder
aka "Mr. RaRa"

$12.95

PURCHASE HERE:
DeployPredatorSurveillance.com

167

NOTES

www.ingramcontent.com/pod-product-compliance
Lightning Source LLC
Chambersburg PA
CBHW060851280326
41934CB00007B/1003